Volume 2

LINDEMANN GROUP

Peter Schiessl

I0427469

Microsoft

WORD 2021

SECOND VOLUME
Training Book
with Exercises

REQUEST EXERCISE TEXTS FOR THIS BOOK BY EMAIL: post@kamiprint.de

ISBN 979-8-882701-74-0
Print on Demand since 2023 in several editions
Translated into English (US) by Peter Schiessl
V250423 / Lindemann Group

Publisher: Lindemann BHIT, Munich
Postal address: LE/Schiessl, Fortnerstr. 8, 80933 Munich, Germany
E-Mail: post@kamiprint.de / Telefax: 0049 (0)89 99 95 46 83
© MSc. (UAS) Peter Schiessl, Munich, Germany
www.lindemann-beer.com / www.kamiprint.de

This book was created from a full installation of MS Office 2021. Deviations from
the descriptions and illustrations are possible due to a user-defined installation or
changes due to other installed software or as a result of updates.

Table of Contents

1. Preface

The structure of this three-part book series should enable you to learn MS Word excellently and step by step without the usual frustration experiences.

You have already seen in the first volume that many things are possible with Word, such as WordArt, Tables, and Tabs or the different Colors for Text or Frames. This training has to be especially systematic because Word offers so many possibilities.

1.1 The three steps to Wordiness

1st Book	2nd Book	3rd Book
Introduction to Word Operation and Program structure, Basic word processing (Font and Paragraph settings), Text design with frames, Color, Numbering and Enumerations, Tabs and Tables, Spell checking, Hyphenation, WordArt …	*An advanced word processor* with Style sheets, Headers, Footnotes, Table of Contents, Basic deepening, Drawing, Insert graphics, Tables, Search and Replace, Business cards, Serial letters, and Labels.	*Word for specialists:* Different Headers or Footers in one Text, Table of Contents, Index, Automatic Numbering, Create your own Dictionaries, Efficient Working with Shortcuts, Sentence Basics, Split Large Documents, More Macros …
Course objective: To make short texts appealing, e.g. a business letter or a birthday invitation.	*Course objective:* Longer texts can be effectively edited and designed, e.g. an annual report or a three-column circular.	*Course objective:* Perfectly design Brochures, Presentations or Doctoral Theses with Index and different Headers.

Please note our special editions:

♦ Serial letters/labels*. The respective material was compiled from volumes 2 and 3 and expanded by additional exercises.

♦ How to create Websites with Word is described in our book "Creating a Homepage with MS Word XX"[1].

---

[1] Once available, the books are offered on www.amazon.com

1.2 About this Volume

◆ Text processing for advanced users means that extensive texts are processed. The most important topics of this volume are therefore

↳ the style sheets as an indispensable basis for formatting (=adjusting) longer texts. In addition, an automatic table of contents can only be generated using style sheets.

◆ For the daily use, it is worthwhile to individually adjust Word, e.g. add new symbols or adjust the automatic saving or the intended storage location, etc.

◆ And then, of course, there are the practical functions that are essential for professional documents:

↳ Automatically create Table of Contents, set Headers, automatic Page Numbering, Footnotes, Source References, a Macro, Serial Letters, Labels, etc.

> In this book, more is described than can be done in a course. Style sheets, Headers and Footers, Footnotes and Endnotes, Cross-references and Serial Letters/Labels should be the basic framework.

1.3 Test your knowledge

Answer the following questions so that you know which course or book is best for you:

◆ Can you write a business letter and set the font and size? Have you ever placed a paragraph in a frame or changed the text color? Do you have any problems with tables and tabs?

↳ These basics are covered in Volume 1. If you have mastered these functions, then Volume 2 is the right choice for you.

◆ Can you reformat a multi-page text with style sheets? Have you already successfully created and adopted a table of contents? Are you familiar with Footnotes and Endnotes, Search and Replace, how to insert graphics, and how to customize toolbars?

↳ Then Volume 3 will be very interesting for you.

Note: ....
....
....
....
....
....
....
....
....
....
....
....

Part One

Style Sheets

the key to professional word processing

You don't have to write exercise texts. Request the exercise texts by email: post@kamiprint.de - please indicate the name given when ordering and the platform through which this book was ordered.

2. Styles

2.1 What are Styles?

In the first volume, you learned how to work with Word and how to manually insert short texts.

- ◆ This method is too cumbersome for longer texts. For a 30-page report with 22 headings, you would have to select each heading and set a larger font, bold, numbering, distance before/after.

  - ✎ It would be a time-consuming business if it weren't for the Style sheets.

- ◆ This is because these formats only need to be saved once in the so-called Style Sheet.

- ◆ The style sheets are then assigned to the paragraphs and with all the settings in place.

One takes advantage of the fact that each text is usually made up of the same elements:

- ◆ Title on the Cover page,

  - ✎ The Cover page only appears once. Here style sheets are therefore completely unnecessary so that everything can still be adjusted manually (selecting and adjusting).

The actual text usually consists of several headings and the text in between, e.g:

- ◆ Heading 1 = Chapter heading,

- ◆ Heading 2 = Subheading,

- ◆ Heading 3 = small Subheading,

- ◆ Body text and normal = the normal Writing text.

In addition, each text contains some specially formatted paragraphs for enumerations, quotations, or text to be highlighted:

- ◆ Quote or indented for text to be highlighted.

These are the same as the names of the style sheets so that, for example, the style sheet heading 1 is only set up once and assigned to all main headings during writing. Further templates can be added as desired.

Advantages of Styles:

- ◆ Even texts of any length can be formatted differently at any time with minimum effort!

  - ↳ This is the only way to ensure good Design or Adaptation to other print media.

  - ↳ If, for example, you want a different font for the chapter headings, the change is only made once in the Heading 1 style sheet and all headings are changed uniformly throughout the text!

> If you overlook a paragraph, for example, or if after a few pages the settings are no longer in the right mind, then different settings can be avoided.

Styles are available in any better word processor, but with different names, such as styles, print styles, paragraph layout, print layout and so on.

2.2 Styles and Paragraphs

Style sheets usually apply to a paragraph. The next paragraph can have the same or a different style.

That is why the distinction between

- ◆ Paragraph mark (¶ by [Return]) and

- ◆ Line break (↵ [Shift]-[Return]) is very important,

so you should make the paragraph marks (¶) visible:

- ◆ with the icon or on the File/Options tab, then to Display:

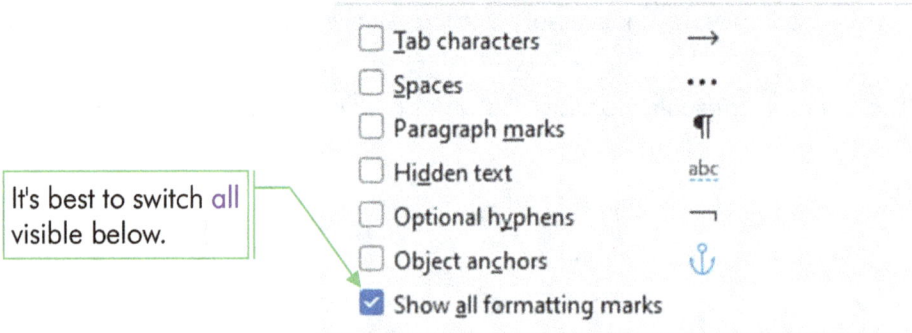

Always show these formatting marks on the screen

☐ <u>T</u>ab characters	→
☐ <u>S</u>paces	•••
☐ Paragraph <u>m</u>arks	¶
☐ Hi<u>d</u>den text	abc
☐ Optional h<u>y</u>phens	⌐
☐ Object an<u>c</u>hors	⚓
☑ Show <u>a</u>ll formatting marks	

It's best to switch all visible below.

Please note the following:

- ◆ Styles apply to the selected Text if the Text has been selected.

- ◆ If, however, only the cursor in the paragraph flashes but no text is selected, the style template automatically applies to the entire paragraph!

> *Therefore, do not select text when assigning a Style sheet!*

2.3 Exercise Styles

You can request the exercise texts informally by email: post@kamiprint.de

➢ Open the file StyleSheets.

2.3.1 Save

> Since this document on your computer comes from an external source, editing it will most likely not be possible initially as additional protection against viruses and malware.

➢ Activate Edit (yellow message at the top of Word).

Save as early as possible:

➢ To avoid overwriting the original exercise, e.g. to be able to start again later, select "File/Save as" and specify a different storage location,

➢ e.g., a newly created folder "Exercises Word 2021 - Second Volume" as a subfolder in your Documents folder.

2.3.2 Assign Styles

➢ Set the Title manually. A Style Sheet offers no advantage, as it only occurs once. So simply mark it, choose a large font and possibly another font.

The Standard Style Sheets, Headings 1, 2 and 3 already exist for this text and for almost every other text. The style sheets for the headings only need to be assigned. This is very simple:

➢ Click once in the first Heading.

Here you have the Standard Style Sheets for quick selection alongside Headings 1, 2 and 3.

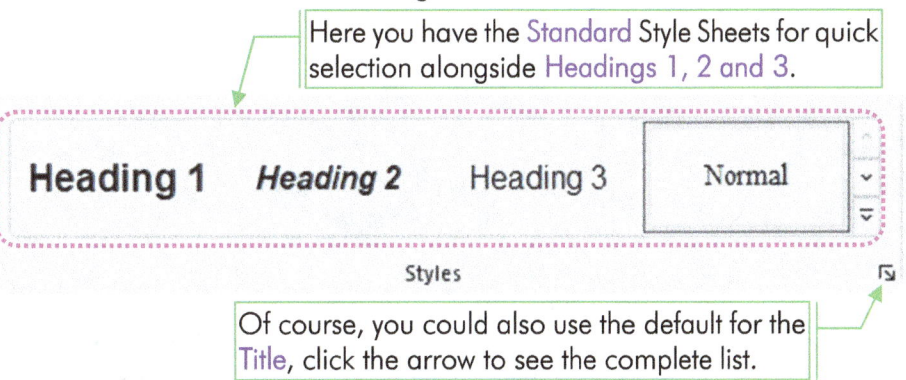

Of course, you could also use the default for the Title, click the arrow to see the complete list.

Select Heading 1. The text automatically adopts the settings of the Heading 1 Style Sheet and should look like this:

Click on the heading, follow the text and observe how the respective style sheet is displayed on top at Styles.

Heading 1

Text - text -

text - text – text.

> ➢ Assign the Headings in the rest of the text to the Headings 1, 2, and 3 style sheets (see the notes in brackets in the exercise text).

2.3.3 Set Styles

We have assigned the default Styles. Now we will set them differently.

> ➢ Click on the heading1 as we want to adjust its styles.

Note: it is recommended to first click on the paragraph that you want to modify. This prevents you from accidentally editing another style because the correct style is already selected in the menu.

Then press here the right mouse button and

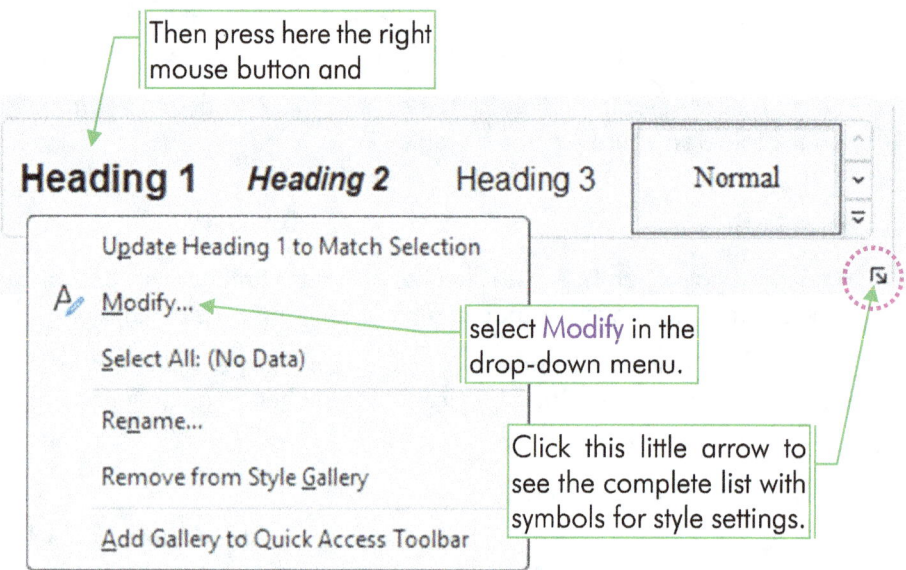

select Modify in the drop-down menu.

Click this little arrow to see the complete list with symbols for style settings.

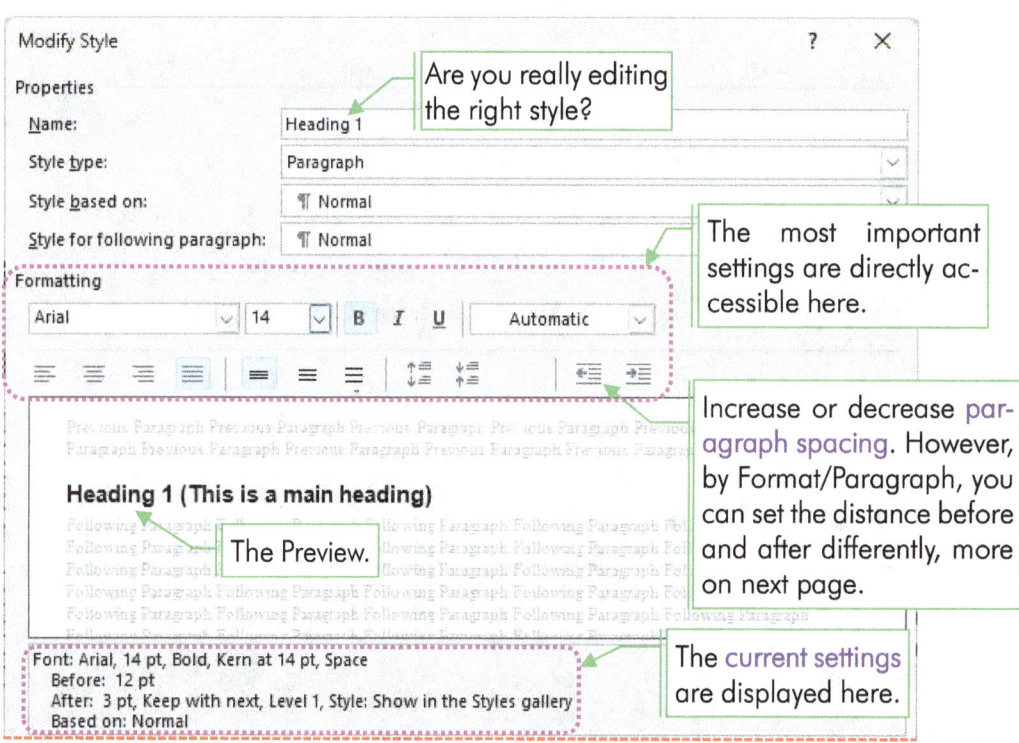

Are you really editing the right style?

The most important settings are directly accessible here.

Increase or decrease paragraph spacing. However, by Format/Paragraph, you can set the distance before and after differently, more on next page.

The Preview.

The current settings are displayed here.

At the bottom of the paragraph menu you find important options:

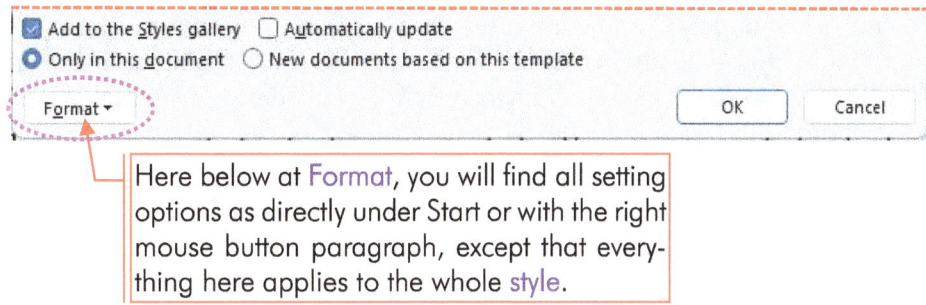

Here below at Format, you will find all setting options as directly under Start or with the right mouse button paragraph, except that everything here applies to the whole style.

The Format button displays this drop-down menu:

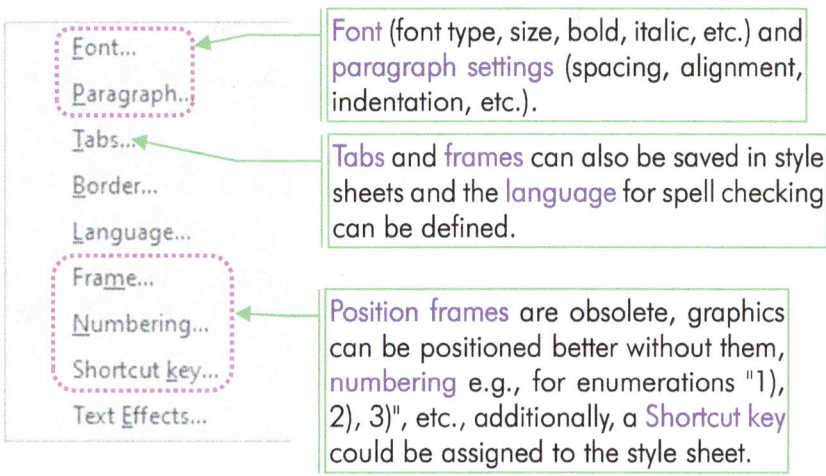

Font (font type, size, bold, italic, etc.) and paragraph settings (spacing, alignment, indentation, etc.).

Tabs and frames can also be saved in style sheets and the language for spell checking can be defined.

Position frames are obsolete, graphics can be positioned better without them, numbering e.g., for enumerations "1), 2), 3)", etc., additionally, a Shortcut key could be assigned to the style sheet.

Set the Heading 1 style sheet as follows:

➢ Font Arial Black, 22 pt, locked 2pt (font style..., the lock goes there on the index card Advanced), text color dark blue,

➢ Enter paragraph spacing before 24 pt, following 6 pt (paragraph...), then switch to line spacing "Simple", if not already set,

➢ Line below with distance 3 pt (frame..., the distance for options), also dark blue.

➢ Delete the note text: (This is the main Heading).

➢ Close the menu, scroll through the text and observe how all paragraphs with the style heading 1 have been changed uniformly.

These basic formattings themselves were described in detail in the first volume.

➢ Now also set the different font, font size and color for the Normal style sheet (= the normal text paragraphs, in some documents, according your Word version, named Standard) and examine the effects.

Please be aware of this:

- So far you have changed the previously marked text "by hand" with the right mouse button/font, paragraph, etc. The same setting options can be found here, but the changes apply here to the style, i.e. to all text paragraphs with this style.

> No matter how long your text is, you can use the styles to change all paragraphs uniformly at any time.

2.4 Exceptions allowed

However, exceptions are also possible.

- You can still select each paragraph and set it differently.
  - ✎ However, these settings will no longer be updated when changes are made to the style.

> Therefore, if possible, you should avoid changing paragraphs manually (select and adjust).

Only if "Automatically update" is checked, no exceptions can be set, since each setting automatically applies to the entire style. This is described in the next main chapter.

2.5 Style is based on

Style sheets can also be built on top of each other to make setting work even more efficient. The subordinate styles first receive all the settings of the main template. For instance, this can be useful for creating two formatting lines, one for the headings and one for all text paragraphs.

- In this case, for example, only the font size and the spacing for each subordinate heading must be set slightly smaller for the headings.
  - ✎ If you select a different font for heading 1, it will also be changed for the subordinate styles for the headings.
  - ✎ If you select a different font for heading 2, this only applies to Heading 2 and if you later change the font for style sheet heading 1, heading 2 will not be changed.

2.6 The practical thing about the styles

- One equals 1,000! You only need to change the style once, and all paragraphs with this style will be updated.
  - ✎ The prerequisite for creating longer texts. Errors caused by forgotten paragraphs that have not been changed can thus be avoided.
- If possible, format only using style sheets! Individual cases can still be set manually. These exceptions will remain if you change the style!

3. Set Up and Update

3.1 Set Up Style Sheets

➢ Now assign Heading 2 in the text and open the menu for the Style Sheets again, this time with a small change:

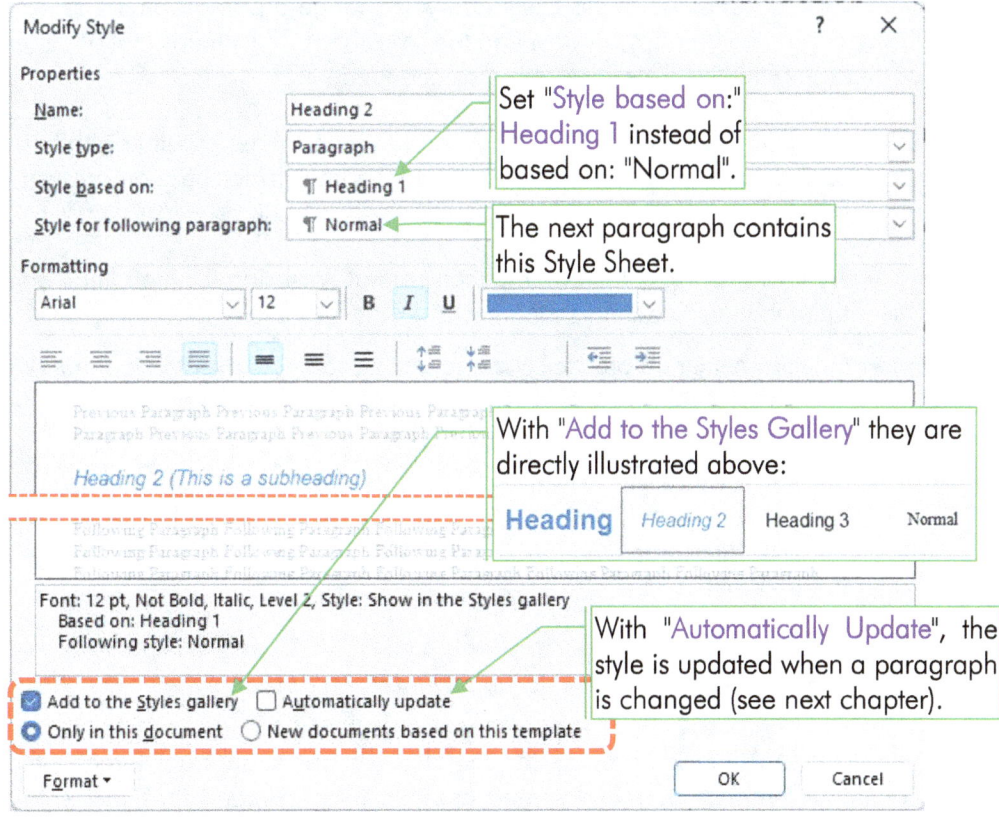

With "Style sheet based on Heading 1", and all settings are taken over from the Style sheet Heading 1.

♦ If you later select a different font for Heading 1, the font is automatically adopted for Headings 2, 3, etc., as these are based on Heading 1.

➢ Only the differences between the Headings need to be set.

This gives us two Stylesheet-Lines since we usually use one font for the text and a thicker one for the Headlines:

    ✎ Heading 1 - Heading 2 ... (based on heading 1),
    ✎ Default - Quote - Enumeration (based on default).

Format the Headings:

➢ Set the font for the style sheets Heading 2 and 3 to a slightly smaller font and deactivate the underline.

➢ Finally, set the text using the Default style: other fonts, 11 pt, justification, single-line, space before and after 3 pt.

3.2 Style sheet for the following paragraph

If "Style for following paragraph" is set to e.g. Body Text, Body Text is automatically assigned after Return. Usually, a normal text paragraph follows a Heading, so that you don't have to change the Style manually.

3.3 Automatically Update

This function (see illustration on the previous page) can save you having to go to the Style sheet menu. If this is set and you change a paragraph in the text, this change is automatically applied to the style sheet. This means that all other paragraphs with this Style sheet are also changed.

> Exceptions for an individual paragraph are no longer possible with this setting, e.g. if a particularly long Heading is to be compressed somewhat.

➢ Try it out: activate the automatically update function for Headings and then change Headings manually.

➢ Check whether automatic Hyphenation is enabled: Layout/Hyphenation.

3.4 New docs that are based on this template

Each document is based on a document template, a file with the name normal.dotx. For each new document, the initial settings (font, styles, etc.) are taken from this file.

☑ Add to the Styles gallery   ☐ Automatically update
◉ Only in this document   ◯ New documents based on this template

With "New documents based on this template", changes are transferred to the document template normal.dotx and apply to all documents that you restart later.

♦ No text will be changed retroactively, as this would have catastrophic consequences if all existing texts were changed.

A simpler, but proven possibility to do without document templates is the method with "Save As".

♦ Set the first document perfectly, e.g. the first letter, then open the first document with the second letter and with File/Save As immediately save under another name.

↳ This gives you a copy with identical settings, the texts can then be overwritten.

4. Additional Style Sheets

4.1 A new Style Sheet

Now comes the quote for which there is no style sheet yet.

➢ Format a paragraph Quote by hand as usual:
  ➢ italic, text color dark red,
  ➢ Indented left and right by one centimeter (ruler),
  ➢ Spacing before and after 18 pt, a single line spacing,
  ➢ Frame with shading as well as space to text
    3 pt (options) of the color red,
  ➢ fine double line, 5% filling (file card
    shading with patterns).

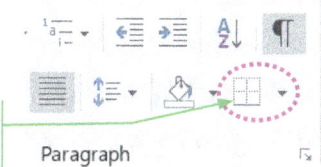

Select "Borders and Shading" at the bottom of the screen to enter the settings menu.

➢ When done, open the menu with the extension arrow for styles and click on the button "New style" below:

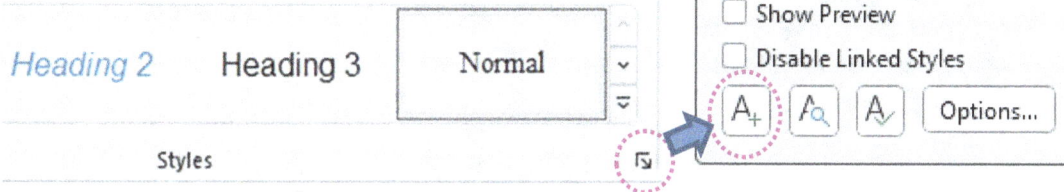

➢ In the window that appears, enter MyQuote as Name, because the paragraph you set was clicked on, its settings are already included in the new format template.

So simply create the format template with OK and now it can be assigned to other quotations using the quick format template bar at the top of Word.

After a quote, the further text usually follows. Therefore, right-click, change and select Body Text or Normal for the following paragraph.

AaBbCcl AaBbCcD AaBbCcD
¶ Heading 3 ¶ My Quote ¶ Normal

Styles

➢ Format the text extensively using Style sheets.

> Note: A Style Sheet is only created once, then it can be assigned or changed as often as desired. So don't re-create it anymore, just assign the newly created style "My Quote" to the other quotations!

Heading 2

Text - Text -

> *Quote - Quote*

Text - Text -

This paragraph occurs only once, therefore press the icon right-justified (=format by hand).

Dr. K. H. Smith-Sample

4.2 Existing Style Sheets

We want to create an Enumeration using a Style sheet.

➢ Find the enumeration paragraphs in the exercise text and try to create a new Style sheet called **Bullets**.

✍ Unfortunately, Word reports that this style sheet already exists although it is not displayed.

Open the Styles menu with the small arrow extension:

Styles

The Bullets Style sheet is not yet displayed.

This list is also very useful for selecting a style sheet and can therefore always remain displayed because clicking on a style sheet assigns it to the current paragraph.

Click here to adjust the display.

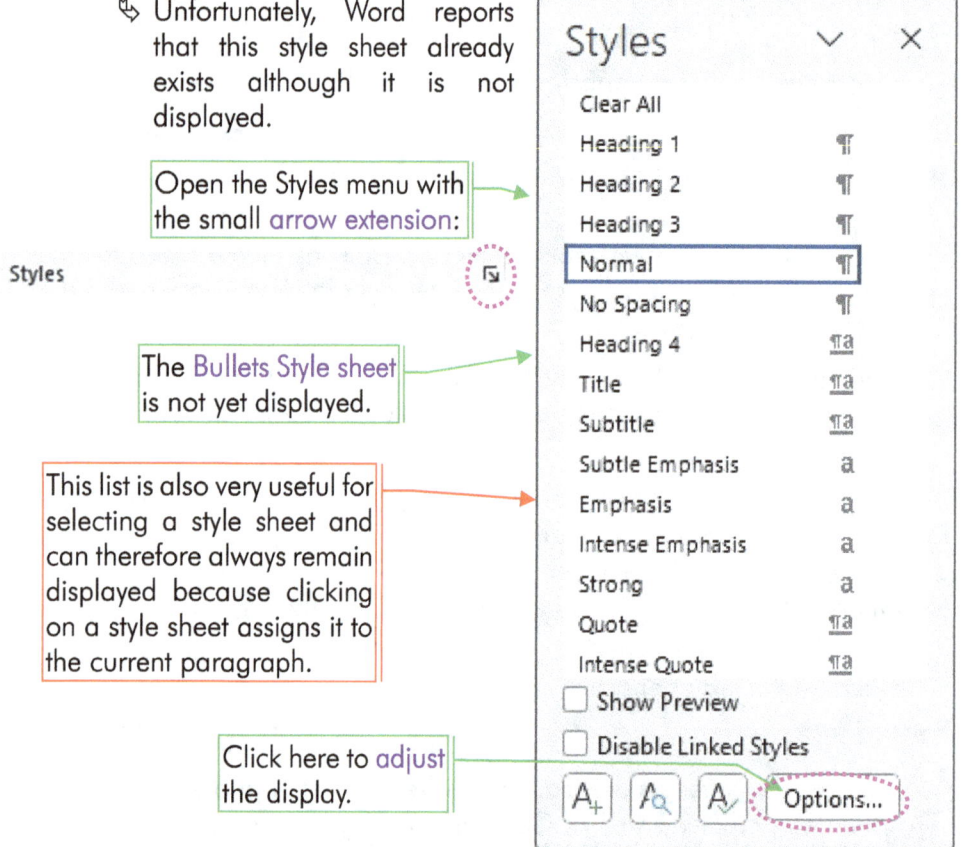

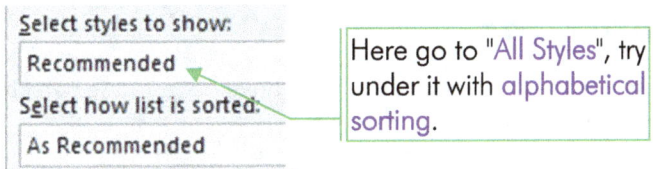

Here go to "All Styles", try under it with alphabetical sorting.

Bottom line: there are already more Style sheets created in Word. Only the recommended or used templates are normally displayed so that it does not become too confusing.

Normally, only the Style sheets used in the current document should be displayed so that the selection is as clear as possible.

➢ Enable All styles and assign the bulleted character style to a bulleted paragraph.

➢ Then switch back to Display: "In current document". Now, this Style is also displayed, because it is used in the text.

➢ Assign the style to the other enumerated paragraphs.

That was good for practice, especially to get to know the other style sheets that already existed.

The Style sheet can be assigned or changed in the menu:

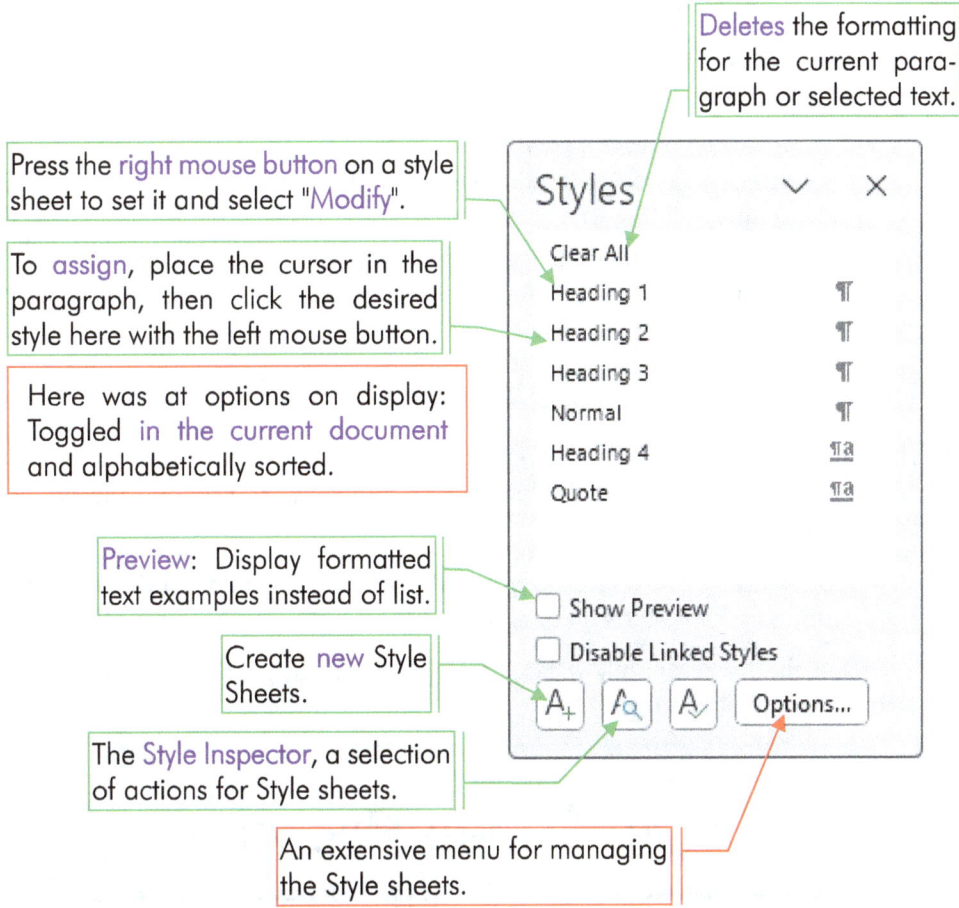

Deletes the formatting for the current paragraph or selected text.

Press the right mouse button on a style sheet to set it and select "Modify".

To assign, place the cursor in the paragraph, then click the desired style here with the left mouse button.

Here was at options on display: Toggled in the current document and alphabetically sorted.

Preview: Display formatted text examples instead of list.

Create new Style Sheets.

The Style Inspector, a selection of actions for Style sheets.

An extensive menu for managing the Style sheets.

4.3 The Format Inspector

The Format Inspector displays whether manual settings have been made, which could be reset here, but would work with [Ctrl]-[Space].

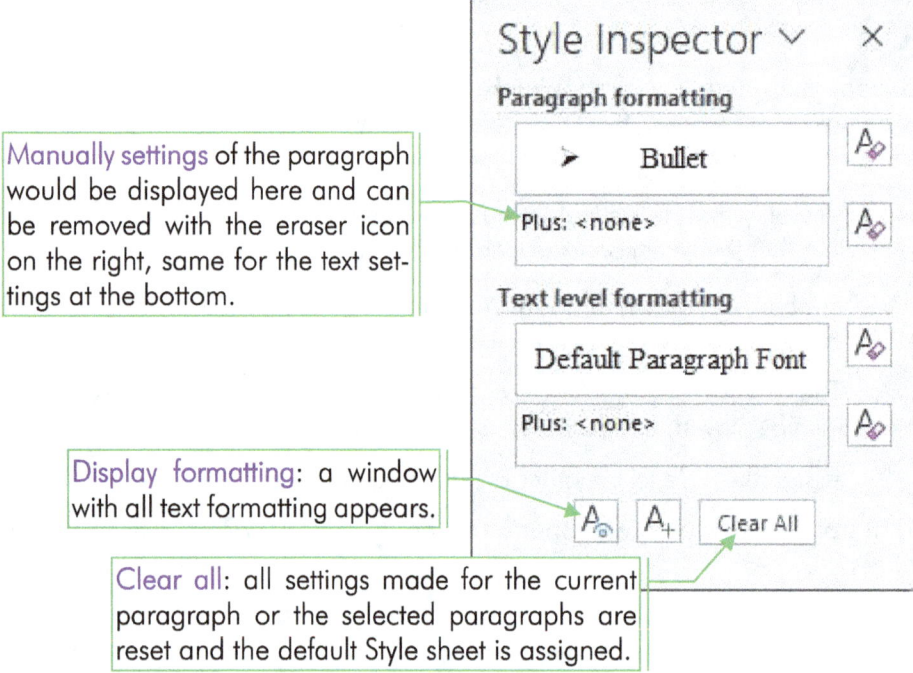

Manually settings of the paragraph would be displayed here and can be removed with the eraser icon on the right, same for the text settings at the bottom.

Display formatting: a window with all text formatting appears.

Clear all: all settings made for the current paragraph or the selected paragraphs are reset and the default Style sheet is assigned.

4.4 Hyperlink

We want to create a Hyperlink to a text on the Internet.

➢ "*You can find further information on the Internet at www.kamiprint.de*".
   As soon as you want to continue writing, MS Word automatically assigns a hyperlink and the Style Hyperlink.

   ✍ The Internet Explorer is opened when you click on the hyperlink while holding down the [Ctrl] key.

4.5 Indent Frames and Lines

The line at heading 1 should only be as long as the text of the heading. You can also set frames and lines for a style, but only as wide as the whole paragraph.

➢ For Heading 1, disable the borderline in the Style menu and choose an underline for Font as an alternative:

➢ Set the title manually without a style sheet: Assign borders, indent left and right in the ruler.

Style Sheets Exercise

➢ Close and save the first text exercise templates.

5. Special Style Sheets

Now we come to the special paragraphs. There are usually some exceptions besides the headings and the normal text, such as the quote in our exercise or enumerations, remarks, exercises, etc. Of course, it is only worthwhile to create a style sheet if a paragraph with these settings appears several times in the text.

But then it is a great advantage to use a style sheet. You can't remember the exact settings even if you only have three Quotes in one text. No problem with the style sheets.

5.1 Hanging Paragraph

In addition to the style sheets mentioned for the headings, the text, and the quote, a hanging paragraph is very common. All other lines hang on the first line. A classic use case is, for example, source references, because it is easier to search for the name.

> ➢ Open the Exercise "SpecialParagraphs" and save as your own in your exercise folder.

> ➢ Assign the style sheet Heading 1 to the title, then Heading 2 to the bibliography.

>> ✋ Also works quickly with the shortcuts [Alt Gr]-1, 2, or 3 for Heading 1, 2, and 3.

>> ✋ If you haven't on your keyboard [Alt Gr] try [Ctrl]-[Alt]-1, 2, 3.

There are several ways to set a hanging paragraph:

♦ Right mouse button on paragraph, then select Paragraph

♦ or or assign a Style, then modify the style to hanging in the Style menu under Format/Paragraph (see p. 17).

♦ As described in the first volume, set in the Ruler with the paragraph sliders.

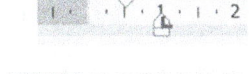

♦ Use the symbol to set an enumeration or numbering, because this automatically sets a hanging paragraph.

> ➢ Click on the paragraph "Müller-Karla...", then open the Styles menu and enter a new Style sheet, as a name "hanging" and proceed to Format/Paragraph.

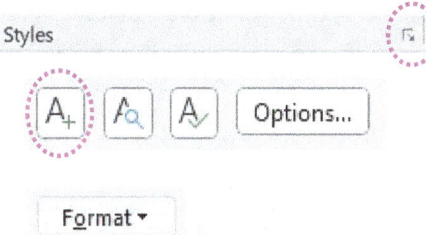

The Paragraph Menu:

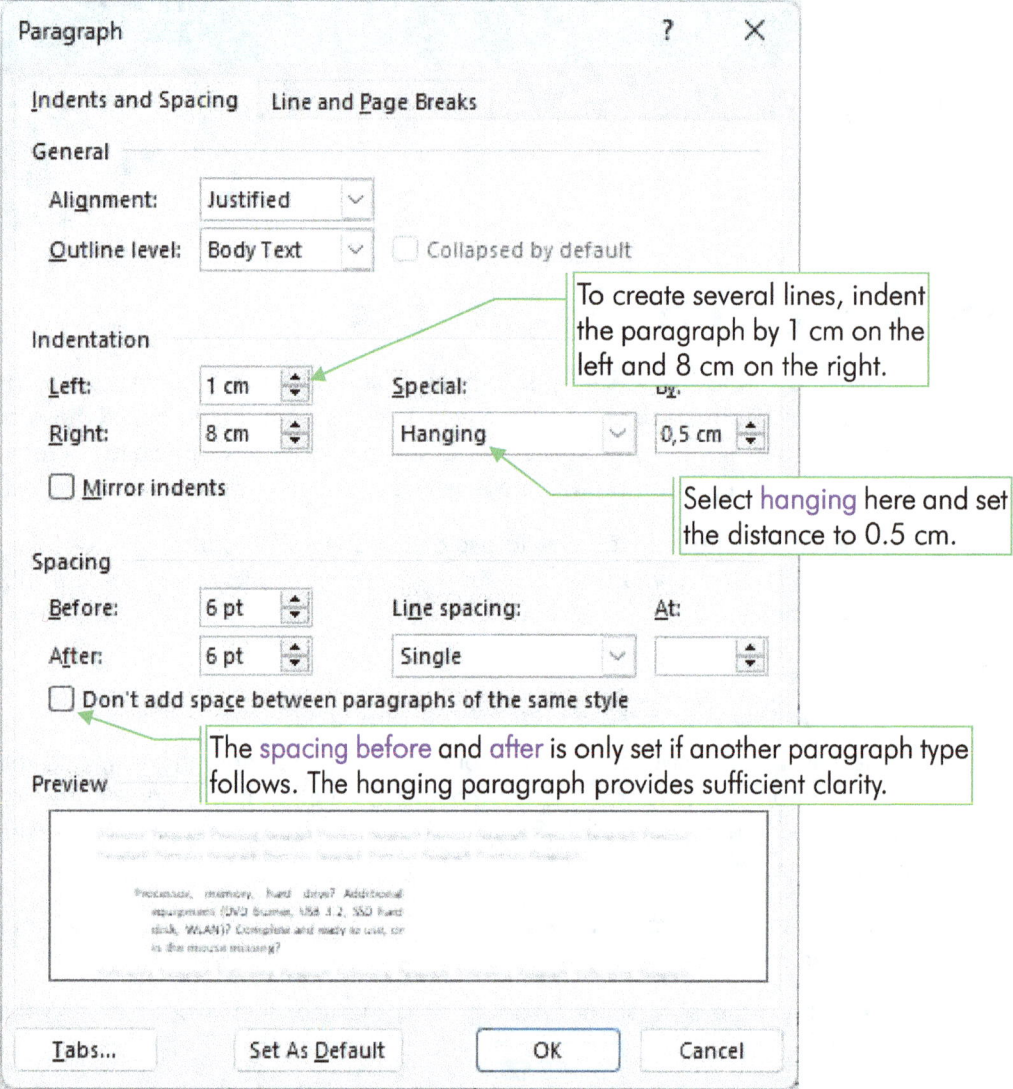

> Select the other paragraphs (e.g. in the left margin) and switch to the new hanging style, which is also displayed directly in the quick style list.

That's the way it should be:

Bibliography[2]

Müller, Karla: Castle stories. A study of Theodor Fontane's work. Munich 1986 (pp. 96-103).

Müller-Seidel, Walter: Theodor Fontane. Social Romance Art in Germany. Stuttgart 1975 (pp. 181-196).

Nuremberg, Helmuth: Theodor Fontane, "Cécile". Unknown sketch for a novel. In: Southgerman newspaper, 11/12 November 1978.

---

[2] Quoted from: Theodor Fontane: Cécile, dtv-Publisher, August 1995, ISBN 3-423-02361-9, p. 276-277 (Computer typesetting and proofreading by Peter Schiessl)

5.2 Numbered Paragraph

The hanging paragraph can also be used for numbering. You will also find this text in the text Exercise named "SpecialParagraphs":

Notepad for computer purchase

1. Processor, Main Memory, Hard Disk? Additional equipment (DVD burner, USB 3.2, SSD hard disk, WLAN)? Complete and ready to use, or is the mouse missing?

2. Big flat screen, at least 24 inches and resolution of at least Full HD 1920*1080, for gamers with a response time under 5ms?

3. Which programs are included, which are needed?

4. How long is the warranty period and will be repaired in the store? How long does a repair take? Is there telephone support?

➢ First, select all paragraphs and quickly assign a number using the Number Icon (see the first Volume).

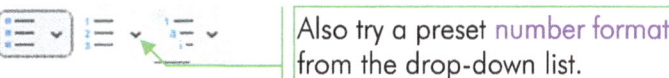

Also try a preset number format from the drop-down list.

◆ Then adjust the settings individually, e.g. indent to the right, larger font size, and other colors, etc.

Although this is very simple, style sheets for enumerations are useful for longer texts: these are formatted one hundred percent identically if there are several enumerations in the text because the same settings of the style sheet apply!

5.3 Arbitrary Bullet Character

Excellent is the possibility to use every special character as a bullet character. You will find enough special characters, for example, in the Windows special font Wingdings (Windows Entity) and Webdings.

➢ You will find the computer shopping list a little further along in the exercise text. For this exercise, we will first create the style sheet Bullet, which will then be assigned to the paragraphs.

➢ Enter Bullet as a name, then select a symbol as enumeration character for Format/Numbering.

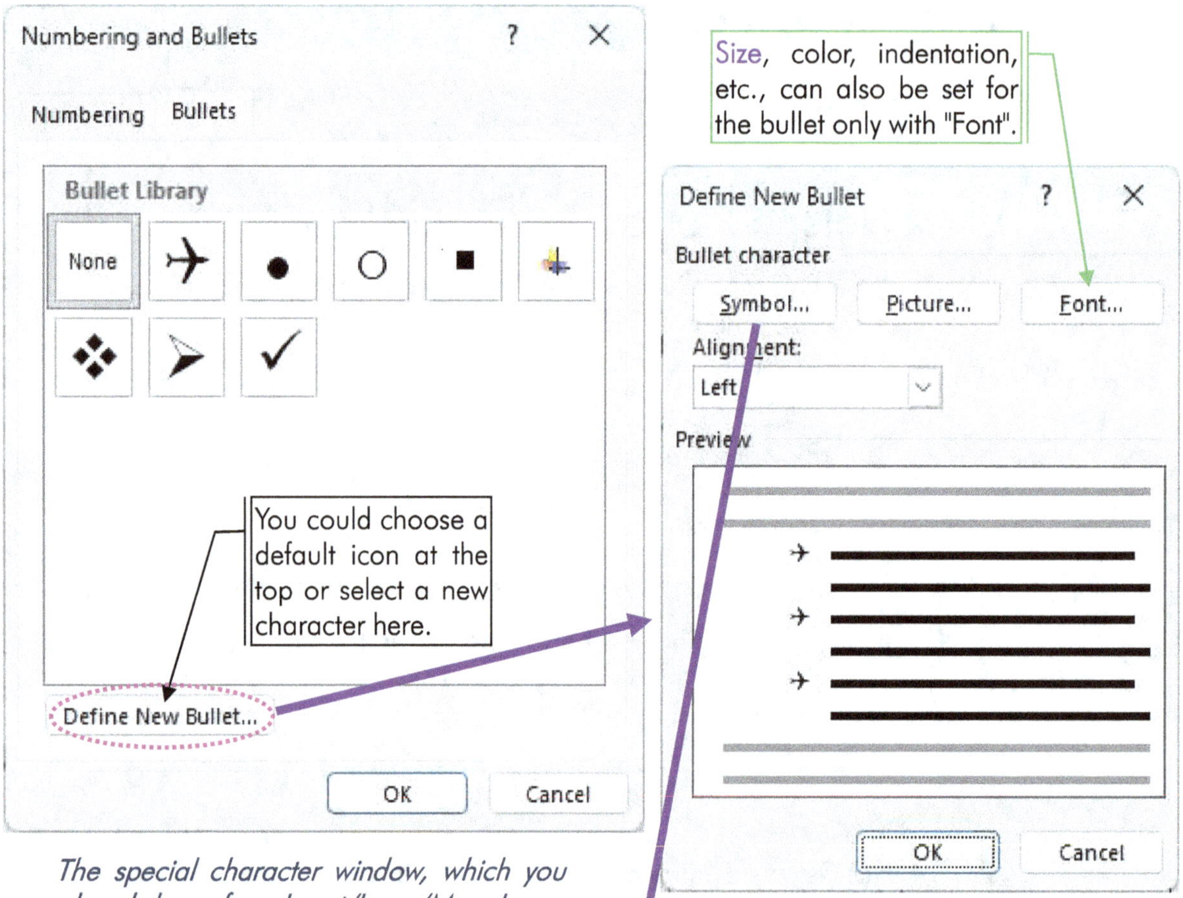

Numbering and Bullets ?   ✕

Numbering   Bullets

Bullet Library

None ✈ ● ○ ◼ ✢

✦ ➢ ✓

You could choose a default icon at the top or select a new character here.

Define New Bullet...

OK   Cancel

Size, color, indentation, etc., can also be set for the bullet only with "Font".

Define New Bullet ?   ✕

Bullet character

Symbol...   Picture...   Font...

Alignment:

Left   ▾

Preview

✈
✈
✈

OK   Cancel

The special character window, which you already know from Insert/Icons/More Icons, will appear for Icons:

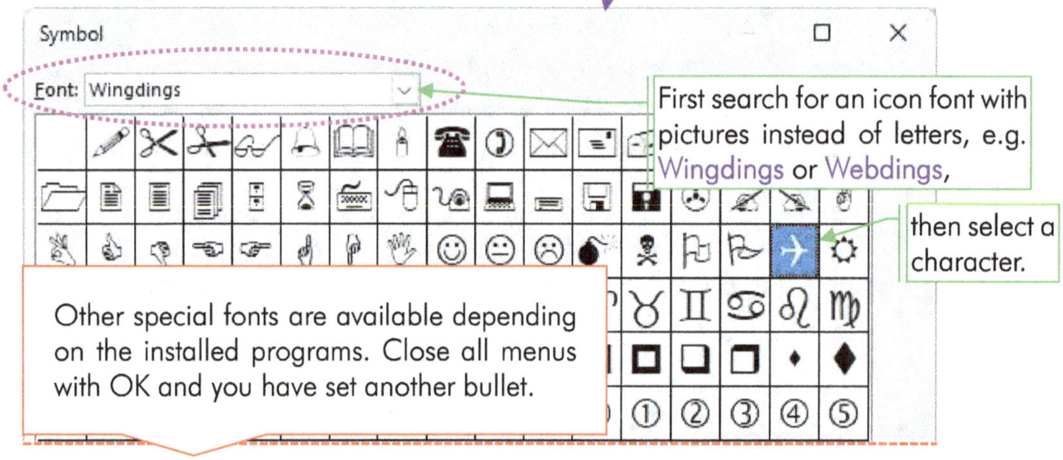

Symbol ▢   ✕

Font: Wingdings   ▾

First search for an icon font with pictures instead of letters, e.g. Wingdings or Webdings,

then select a character.

Other special fonts are available depending on the installed programs. Close all menus with OK and you have set another bullet.

When you assign a numbering or enumeration, a tab is automatically set and the paragraph is indented.

♦ You can also change the indentation using the ruler if you check "Automatic update" in the style sheet:

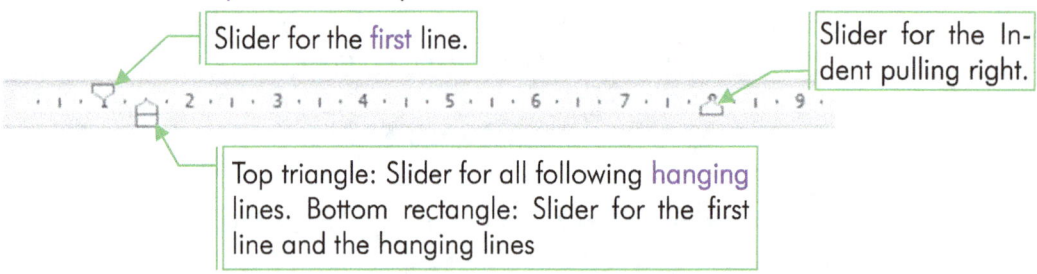

Slider for the first line.

Slider for the Indent pulling right.

Top triangle: Slider for all following hanging lines. Bottom rectangle: Slider for the first line and the hanging lines

6. Printing large Documents

The main settings for printing were presented in the first volume. Now it goes one step further because there are some helpful settings for printing long texts.

You can print in the following ways:

[Ctrl]-p

♦ An icon for printing no longer exists. Instead, use the keyboard shortcut [Ctrl]-p (p for print) or File/Print.

   ✎ The Setting menu appears, in which you can specify the print quality and other print settings.

   ✎ Back or cancel print: See top-left arrow or [Esc].

   ✎ You can set the print preview at the bottom right:

| Use the slider or +/- to zoom in or out. |

| Click here to display the Zoom menu. | 110 % — |

6.1 The Print Sequence

➢ Select [Ctrl-p] to print for any open document, e.g. from the previous exercise "Special".

The Printer is set at the Top:

Print

Copies: 1

Print

| Select the printer here and set the printer properties, e.g., paper type or print quality. |

Printer ⓘ

Microsoft Print to PDF
Ready

Printer Properties

Some Print parameters can also be selected directly in the menu:

| Print the document properties or a list of Style sheet instead of the document. |

Settings

Print All Pages
The whole thing

Pages: ⓘ

| Single pages: 3;8;11 or ranges: 5-12 or mixed: 5;9;14;18-22. |

Print One Sided
Only print on one side of the...

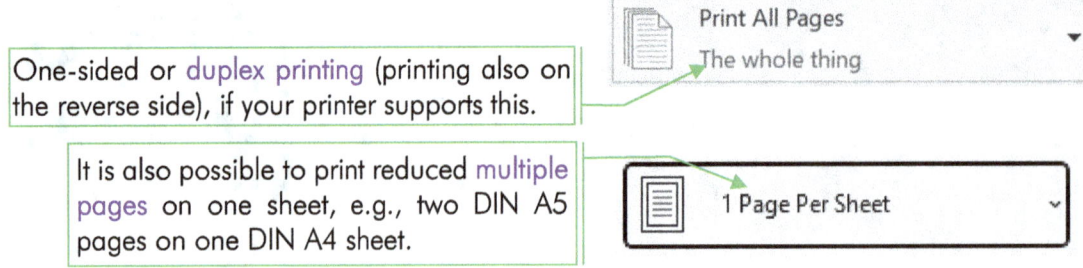

One-sided or duplex printing (printing also on the reverse side), if your printer supports this.

It is also possible to print reduced multiple pages on one sheet, e.g., two DIN A5 pages on one DIN A4 sheet.

6.2 Print Preferences

♦ With File/Options/Advanced right to browse to print, here you can set the Word print options.

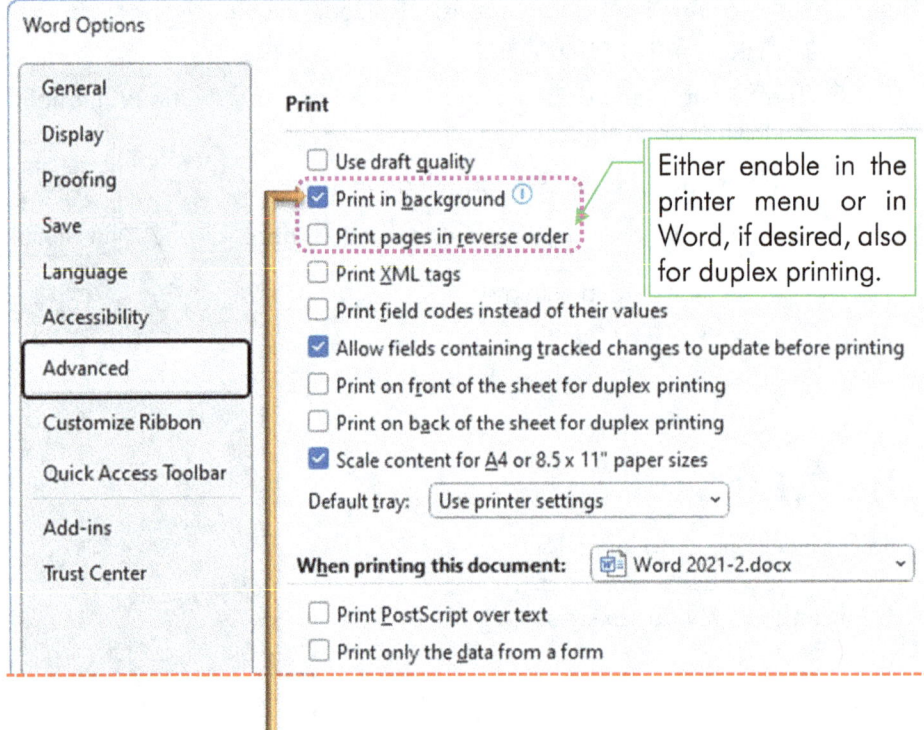

Either enable in the printer menu or in Word, if desired, also for duplex printing.

♦ If "Print in the background" is activated, work can continue immediately while the print is being processed.

♦ Most inkjet printers eject paper with the printed side up.

　↬ Then the last page must be printed first, i.e. with "reverse order", so that the pages are printed in the correct order.

　↬ Most laser printers print in normal print order because the paper is ejected with the printed side down.

♦ Updating fields…: so that, for example, a table of contents will be updated before printing.

Duplicate settings, such as duplex printing in Word and in the printer menu, can cancel each other out.

6.3 Printout in File

These two methods are useful if you want to print a document more often or pass on a print file.

If you have a Postscript printer, you could print to a print file and send the file to a printer or print on many computerized copying machines.

- ♦ Postscript = standardized printer language was developed by Adobe as early as 1980 for the exchange of print data in the professional sector.

- ♦ Alternatively, to print documents on other computers with identical formatting, the file could be output to a pdf document.

  - ✎ In addition to the standard Adobe program, there are also free alternatives on the web.

  - ✎ A printer is installed during the installation of the program on which you can print the document, which is saved as a pdf file.

6.4 Cancel Printing

The following happens very often: the print is sent and you notice another error. It helps if you know how to stop and delete a print job.

> As an immediate help to avoid unnecessary paper waste, simply switch off the printer or even unplug it if it switches on automatically.

As long as Word performs the print processing, a message appears at the bottom right of Word. Double-clicking on it would cancel printing, but today computers are usually so fast that printing is completed in less than a second. Since printing on paper takes longer, the print icon at the bottom right of the Windows start bar is more accessible:

Use the arrow "^" to display further symbols, then right-click on the printer symbol and "Open printer".

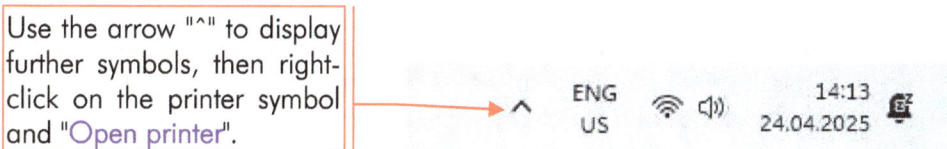

For short documents, the display is usually too short. In any case, you can cancel a printout in the print menu:

- ➢ Open the print menu: Start/Settings/Bluetooth & Devices/Printers & Scanners. Click on the printer there and open the printer queue.

- ➢ No matter how you get to the menu, in the printer's menu you can press the right mouse button on the print job to stop or cancel it, also possible with [Del].

On a computer network, print jobs from others may be in the queue. Pay attention to the "Owner" column and the start time. Print jobs in the queue are often forgotten in networks, for example, because no one has added paper.

6.5 Business Card Exercise

Create the following Business Card:

> ➤ Start a new file, choose page format 6x3cm with 0,4cm margins each (alternatively 3x2" with 0,3"margins), write and center text, choose text color and font, format the font size matching small, then add a horizontal line.

Viola Violina

―――――――――――――

Musician

Violine- Piano - Saxophone

Music lessons by Appointment

Phone: 191 / 1919191919

Of course, specific graphics programs offer the most possibilities. There are also astonishingly many setting options in the text program and the necessary settings for printing.

There are two practical printing alternatives for business cards in Word, the table or label method (or even a graphics program):

- ♦ Create a table (see the first volume) in the size of the business card paper, one cell corresponds to one business card, and copy the first, perfectly arranged card into the other table cells,

  - ✎ which is a little handwork, but the easiest method, which should always work without any problems.

- ♦ Or you can use the mail merge function: Index card shipments, there you can start serial printing/labels.

  - ✎ If you cut the labels yourself, specify your own dimensions using the "New label" button.

  - ✎ If you use prepared label paper with pre-perforated, easy-to-tear labels (available from a specialist retailer), enter your label paper (label manufacturer and type) in the menu that appears.

  - ✎ In the menu that appears, select the label manufacturer and label type or specify your own dimensions using the "New label" button.

There is color pre-printed and pre-perforated paper available in specialist shops for business cards. Text can be printed relatively easily using the table method. Then the business cards only have to be broken out and beautiful business cards are ready.

- ♦ To print, select "thick paper" or cardboard in the printer menu and of course best print quality.

  - ✎ Some inkjet printers have a lever to widen the paper feeder for thick paper.

- ♦ With special spray varnish or laminating devices, the self-created business cards could be made waterproof.

  - ✎ Inkjet prints are usually not waterproof in contrast to laser prints!

Part Two

Setting Word

more comfortable working
through optimal settings

7. The Word Options

Word can be customized to individual needs, such as adding very important commands to the Quick Access toolbar or assigning keyboard shortcuts for other actions.

7.1 Quick Access Toolbar Customization

This allows you to add more Icons to the Quick Access Toolbar:

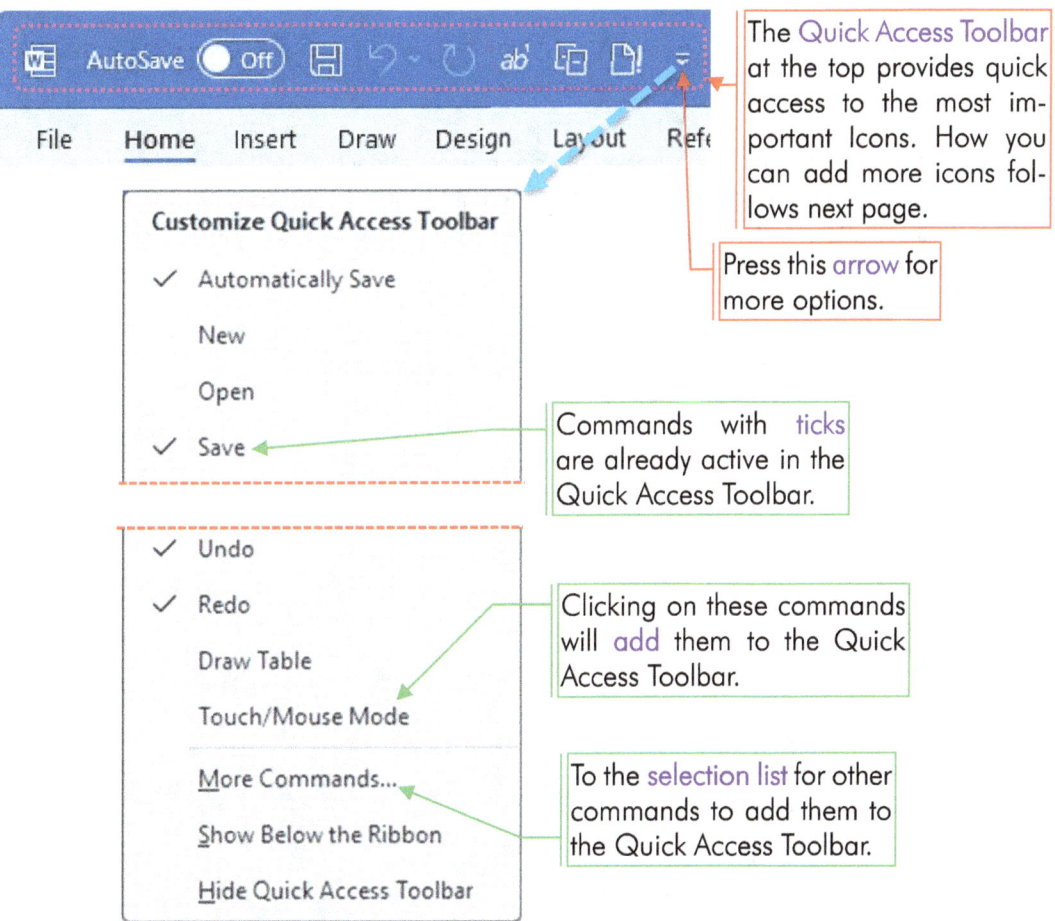

The Quick Access Toolbar at the top provides quick access to the most important Icons. How you can add more icons follows next page.

Press this arrow for more options.

Commands with ticks are already active in the Quick Access Toolbar.

Clicking on these commands will add them to the Quick Access Toolbar.

To the selection list for other commands to add them to the Quick Access Toolbar.

7.1.1 Add New Icons

Assuming you would often have to insert cross-references and footnotes.

Let's save the way to the References tab by adding these two icons to the Quick Access Toolbar.

➢ Select "More Commands..." from the extension arrow:

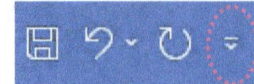

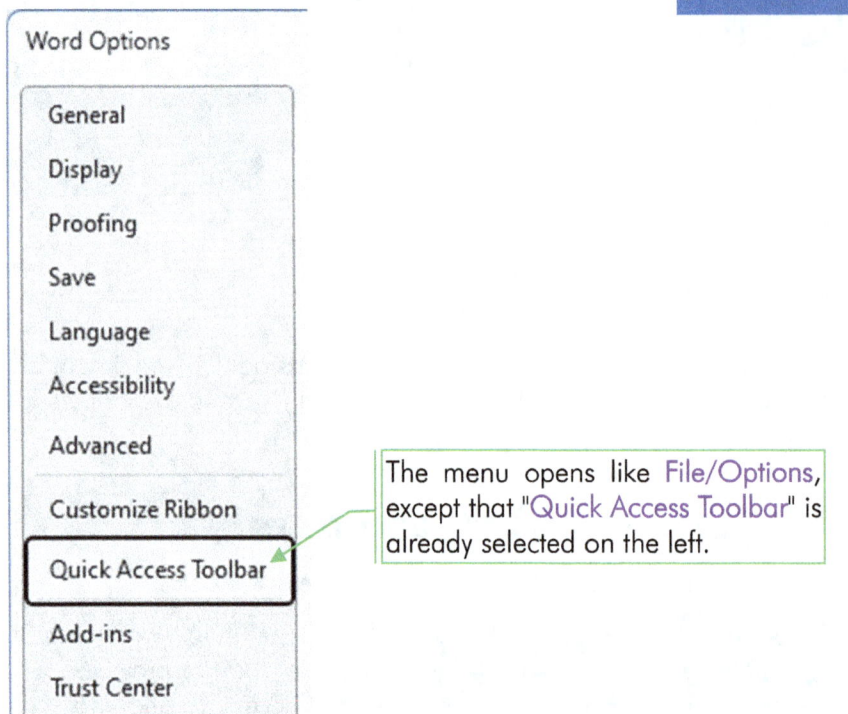

The menu opens like File/Options, except that "Quick Access Toolbar" is already selected on the left.

Since there are an enormous number of commands, it is important to select a suitable tab. There the commands are sorted into groups as above in the command bar: "File – Home/Insert etc.", here using the "References" tab as an example:

The icons are sorted here in a variety of ways, e.g., start, insert, page layout, etc. like the menus above: therefore, select the References tab here.

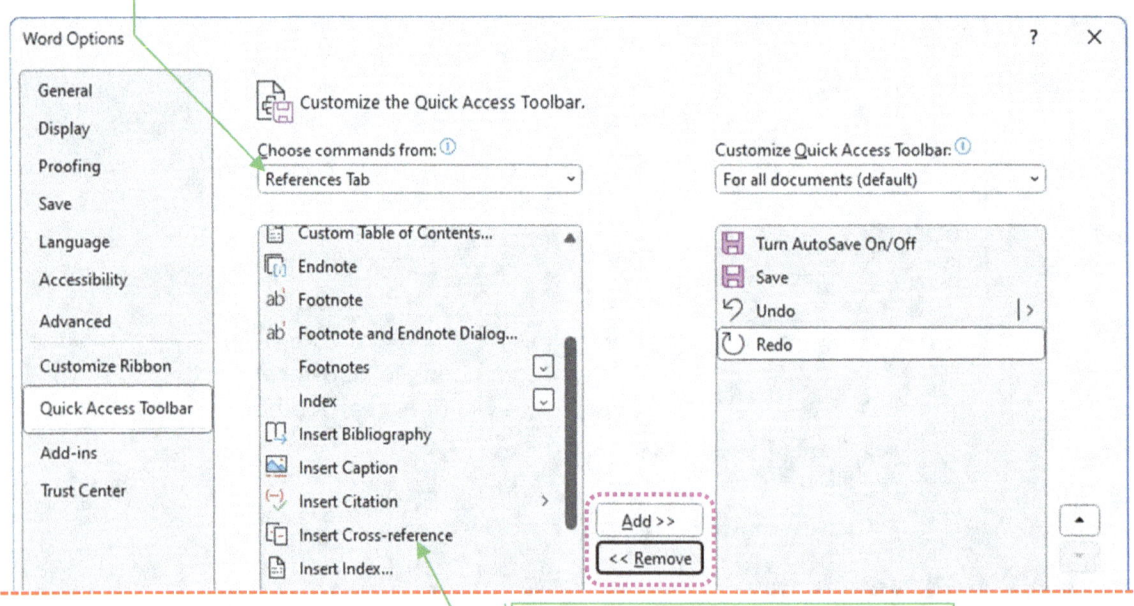

Insert a cross-reference and add a footnote to the quick access selection with the Add button to the right.

➢ The Quick Access Toolbar looks like this after you have added both commands with Add to right:

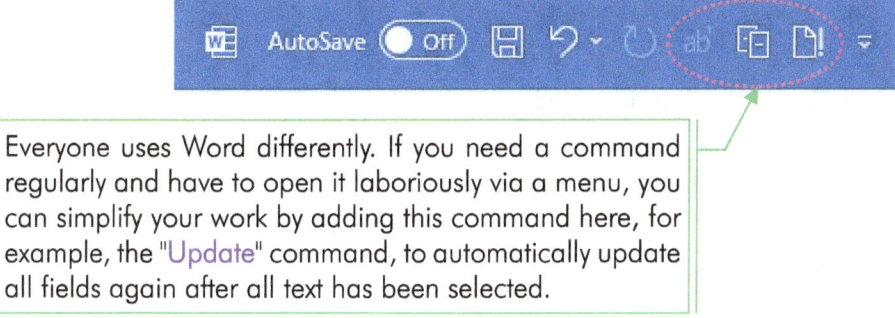

Everyone uses Word differently. If you need a command regularly and have to open it laboriously via a menu, you can simplify your work by adding this command here, for example, the "Update" command, to automatically update all fields again after all text has been selected.

7.2 Set The View

Actually in File/Options, but you can also use the arrow in the quick access bar in the same way with More Commands.

The left side contains some menus, here for "Display" as sample:

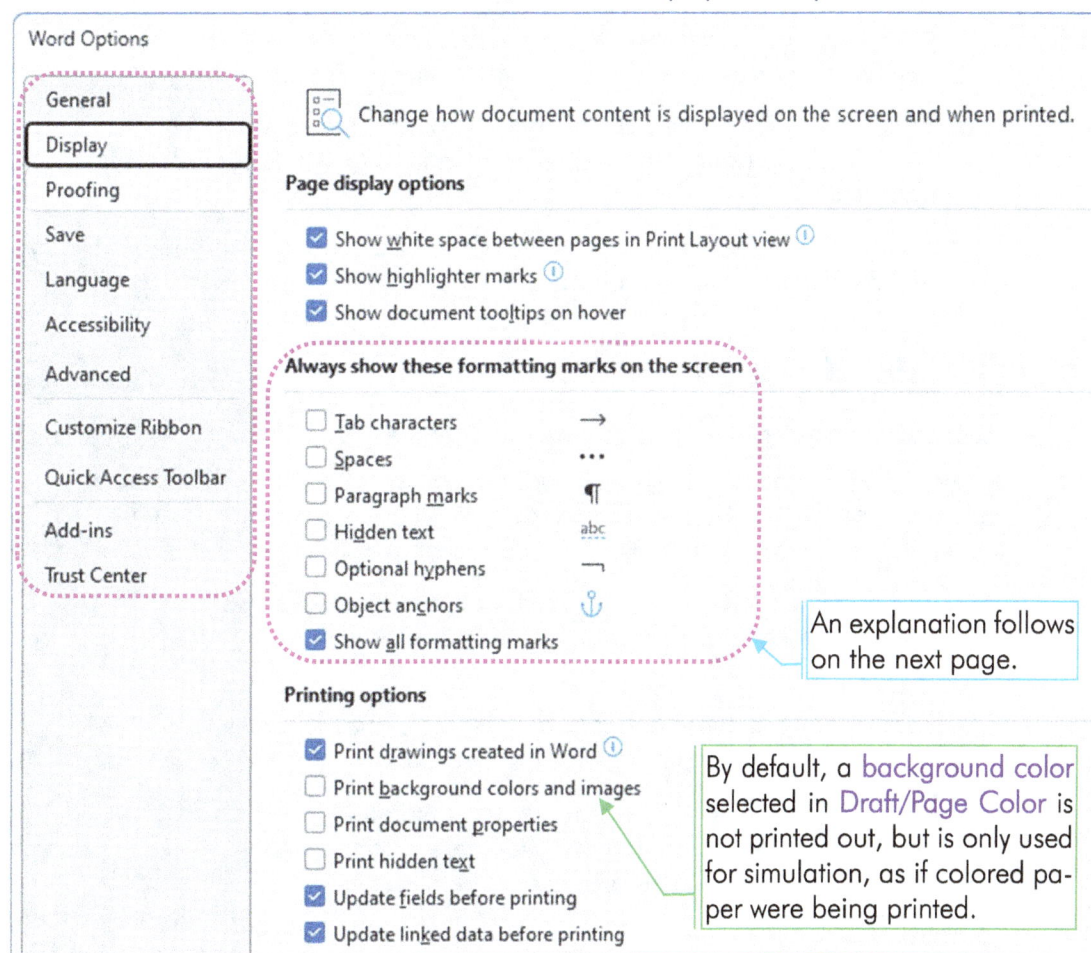

An explanation follows on the next page.

By default, a background color selected in Draft/Page Color is not printed out, but is only used for simulation, as if colored paper were being printed.

7.2.1 The Formatting Characters

These are control characters that are displayed on the screen but are not printed. Here you can choose which formatting characters you want to see:

♦ Errors caused by double tabs (tab stop characters) or spaces can be avoided if these characters are displayed.

♦ Paragraph marks, including line feeds, are extremely important when using style sheets and should, therefore, be visible.

♦ Hidden Text: in order to place the information for a keyword index in the text, the keywords must be written in the text at the appropriate location, but should not be printed there.

   ✍ That's why these are formatted as so-called hidden text, which can be displayed for editing, but is otherwise usually switched off and remains invisible.

   ✍ Further down these could also be for example for correction printouts with printed out, then, of course, the text shifts. More about an Index follows in the third Volume.

♦ Conditional Hyphens are set with [Ctrl]-Dash and are only active if the word is actually hyphenated, so hyphens can be set manually, e.g. if Word hyphens incorrectly without there being any risk of hyphens remaining in the middle of the text after changing the font size.

♦ Object Anchor: an object (AutoForm, photo, etc.) hangs with this anchor on a paragraph and is moved with this shift, e.g. if a text is added in front of it.

All characters can be switched on or off with the adjacent icon in the Start menu. Recommendation: Switch on ALL.

¶

7.3 The Print Options

Formatting characters are followed by these print options:

Refreshing before printing is always good, the background colors should also be printed as a rule, but we usually do not want to print the document properties and the hidden text except for correction purposes.

♦ The document properties can be viewed and entered in File/Info. This box can be ticked if you want to print them for control purposes or to pass them onto paper.

♦ Print hidden text: these are, for example, the entries for a keyword index which could also be printed with this function.

♦ Update fields before printing are for automatic calculations or cross-references. Tick here so that these values are updated and correct before each printout.

♦ Update linked data…: you can insert an object in the Insert menu. An object is a file created in another program, e.g. MS Excel. This file is currently read when the Word document is opened; this file is also refreshed before printing if ticked.

Printing options

- ☑ Print drawings created in Word
- ☐ Print background colors and images
- ☐ Print document properties
- ☐ Print hidden text
- ☑ Update fields before printing
- ☑ Update linked data before printing

7.4 Advanced

Some useful settings are hidden in File/Options/**Advanced**:

General

Display

Proofing

Save

Language

Accessibility

Advanced

Customize Ribbon

Quick Access Toolbar

Add-ins

Trust Center

Show document content

☑ Show background colors and images in Print Layout view

☐ Show text wrapped within the document window

☐ Show picture placeholders ⓘ

☑ Show drawings and text boxes on screen

☑ Show bookmarks

☐ Show text boundaries

☐ Show crop marks

☐ Show field codes instead of their values

Field shading: When selected ▾

☐ Use draft font in Draft and Outline views

Name: Courier New ▾

Size: 10 ▾

Font Substitution...

☐ Expand all headings when opening a document ⓘ

> **Text borders** display the page margin and help to position images.

> **Crop marks** at the edge of the page margin help you trim when printing multiple pages on a larger format.

What needs to be explained here is:

◆ Show text wrapped... only applies to the Design view. The text is displayed with original wraps if ticked up to the edge of the Word window.

◆ Show picture placeholders for graphics instead of the actual graphics saves processing power, but there is enough of that available today.

◆ Show bookmarks are marks in the text to refer to elsewhere by means of a cross-reference and should therefore also be visible when bookmarks are used.

Note: ....

....

....

....

....

....

....

....

....

....

....

....

7.5 Save and Storage Location Setting

➢ In the options menu, switch to Save.

Customize how documents are saved.

Save documents

☑ AutoSave files stored in the Cloud by default in Word ⓘ

Save files in this format:　　　Word Document (*.docx)

☑ Save AutoRecover information every　10　minutes

　☑ Keep the last AutoRecovered version if I close without saving

AutoRecover file location:　　C:\Users\Peter\AppData\Roaming\Microsoft\Word\　　Browse...

☐ Don't show the Backstage when opening or saving files with keyboard shortcuts

☑ Show additional places for saving, even if sign-in may be required.

☐ Save to Computer by default

Default local file location:　　C:\Users\Peter\Documents\　　Browse...

Default personal templates location:　C:\Users\Peter\Documents\Benutzerdefinierte Office-Vorlagen\

◆ The first option, storing files in the cloud (OneDrive or others), offers some advantages, but should also be viewed critically, because without the Internet you have no access, for example if your router fails or the telephone line is disrupted since the Internet is usually transmitted with DSL, you can no longer edit the texts.

　↳ In addition, changes are saved automatically immediately. If you open a text as a template and then make adjustments and want to save it as a new document using File/Save As, this function will have already changed the original document. You can either disable this function and enable "*Save to Computer by default*" below, or save it as a new document using File/Save As before making any changes.

　↳ The cloud is of course ideal for workgroups when several people need to access these files.

◆ Save AutoRecover information...: Here you can set Word to "save changes" for example, every ten minutes.

　↳ If the computer crashes, Word automatically reconstructs the state of this back-up but this is not the current state!

◆ Default local file location: if, e.g., you have your texts on a second hard disk in the texts folder, you would select D:\Texts with Browse.

　↳ If you specify your default folder for Word texts using the "Browse..." button, you don't have to select the folder every time you open or save.

◆ Embed fonts in the file: these are saved in the text file so that the document can also be correctly displayed on computers on which these fonts are not loaded.

　↳ Also fixes the problem that its font may no longer exist on a new computer or operating system.

8. Corrections

8.1 The Spell Checker Menu

Word underlines wrong words instantly. This automatic spell checker is better and more convenient because you can correct mistakes instantly. The Spelling menu is therefore only useful in exceptional cases.

The spellchecker works according to a simple principle. MS Word comes with a dictionary containing thousands of words. Each word is compared with this dictionary. An error message will appear if there is no identical entry.

abc
✓
Spelling & Grammar

♦ You can access the spellchecker as follows:
  ✍ with the icon shown in the Review menu on the left side.
  ✍ or by using the shortcut [F7].

F7

This Docking Window appears:

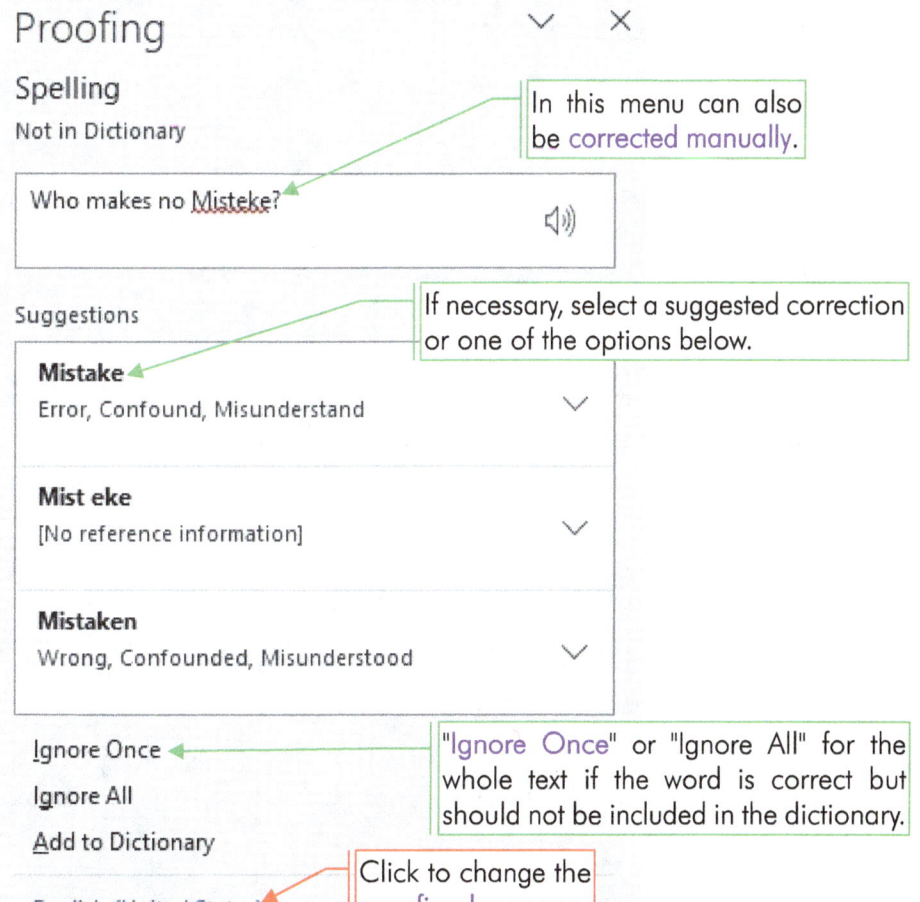

♦ Add to Dictionary:

    ↳ add the current word to the user dictionary.

    ↳ Highly recommended for recurring words such as your name and street.

♦ With this, you can build up an individual dictionary over time.

8.2 Grammar checking

♦ With manual spellchecker, grammar is also checked, so there is no separate menu for grammar checking.

♦ Spelling mistakes are underlined in red, grammar mistakes in a blue double line.

♦ Grammar error in the Document check menu: "Ignore Once" only does not change this expression, with "Ignore All", the underlying grammar rule in this text is never used for checking again.

    ↳ Under Options you can view the grammar rules and deactivate rules, you should take a look at this list.

8.3 Select Language

And that's not just for one language. In addition to country-specific English (GB, USA, Australia, etc.) there are many other languages available.

Write this short text in German language, intentionally making a few mistakes (red marked):

Aktion:	Shortcut:
Aktuelles Dokument ducken	Strg+P
Aktuelless Dokiment schließen	ALT+F4
Zur ersten Seite gehen	Strg+Pos1
Zr letzteen Seite gehen	Strg+Ende
Hilfetäxte anzeigen	F1

➢ Select the foreign-language text, then in the menu Review/Language/Set Proofing Language... select the appropriate language "German" and try to correct the mistakes.

    ↳ You can also tick "Detect language automatically" in this menu, but this does not work for most texts with many technical terms.

Because you only select the language for the selected text, different languages can be specified within a document.

Important note: the language can also be defined in the styles, so that a separate style could be set up for paragraphs in a foreign language.

8.4 Translate

➢ Let's just test to translate: "Es regnet. Ich werde mit meinem Regenschirm zur Arbeit gehen müssen."

✎ First try to translate only the "Regenschirm", right-click it/Translate. Then mark the entire sentence and the translation will automatically be expanded.

✎ The translate menu appers, in which you can choose very much languages as target. The language is usually recognized automatically and if not, select manually in the selection list.

There are also many dictionaries and translation programs on the Internet, just search for dictionary or translation program, the most famous is google translate. However, many automatic translations are currently still incorrect and must be corrected manually.

8.5 The AutoCorrect

The AutoCorrect function corrects default errors while writing which is a useful help but can sometimes cause problems.

➢ Use Right Mouse Button/Add to AutoCorrect is meant for your default errors. The word will be added to the AutoCorrect list and automatically replaced by the suggested correction in the future.

➢ The AutoCorrect function can be found under File/Options, then Proofing/Autocorrect Options:

The upper part is mainly about capitalization:

To begin each sentence with a capital letter means: after each punctuation, even after abbreviations which is why these are noted separately as exceptions.
If MS Word does not recognize an abbreviation, it will automatically be capitalized after the period of the abbreviation.

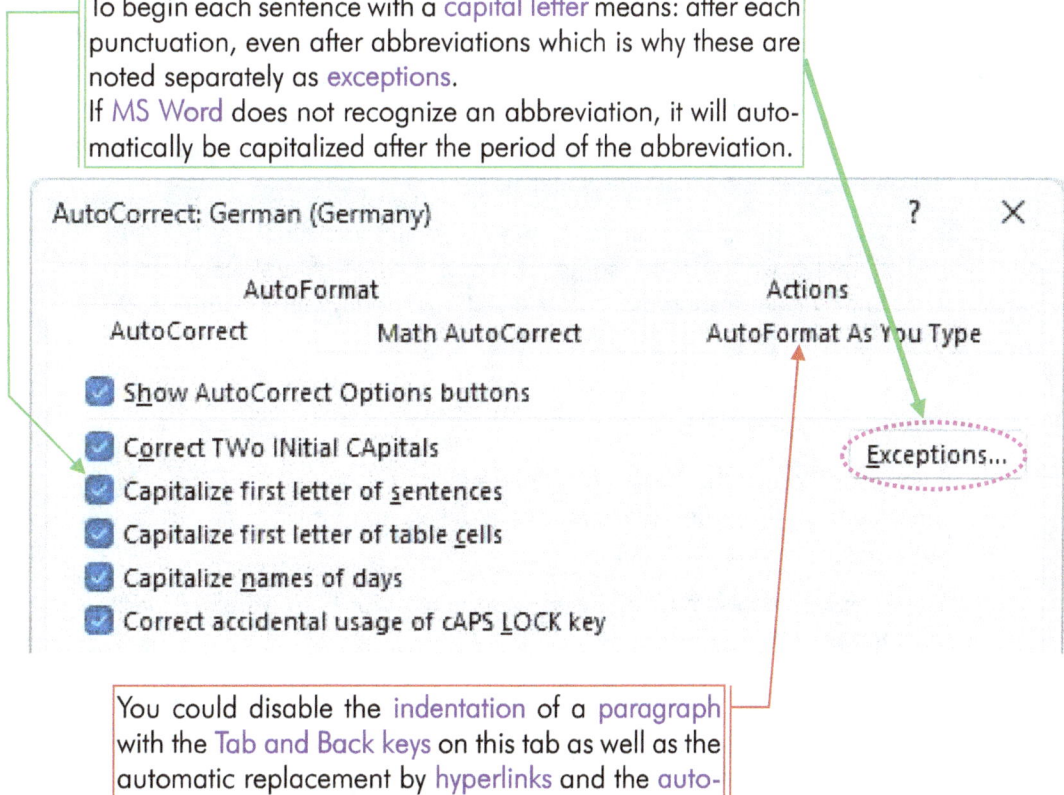

You could disable the indentation of a paragraph with the Tab and Back keys on this tab as well as the automatic replacement by hyperlinks and the automatic numbering if you start paragraphs with 1, 2.

Common errors that are automatically corrected are listed at the bottom:

This means that this menu can be used as a writing aid instead of corrections by entering frequently used, very long or complicated words here and replacing them with an abbreviation.

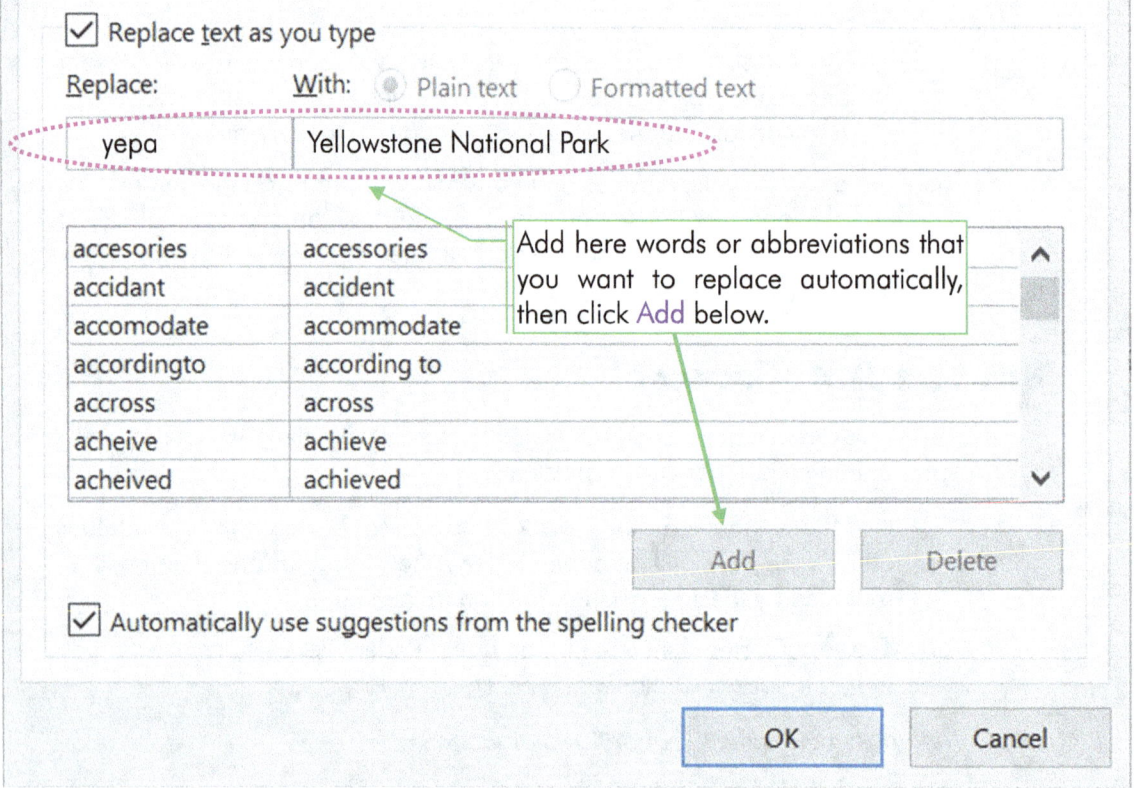

> Try it out with your own long word or the example from the illustration above. After "Replace" and "OK", it is enough to just write "yepa", followed by a space bar, this will automatically be replaced by "Yellowstone National Park" replaced.

> ✎ Of course, this is very similar to the quick building blocks and Auto-Text, but it works in the same way and the list of replacements is definitely clearer than the AutoText settings menu, the building block manager.

More about AutoCorrect:

♦ If you want to use the "Capitalize first letter of sentences" function, you should enter a few more abbreviations in the exceptions list (Exceptions… button) in the course of time.

♦ Some replacements may interfere. Mark such words and delete them from the list.

8.6 Display Corrections

This function has nothing to do with spell-checking or auto-correcting, but rather with highlighting all manual changes made to a text in color. This is particularly useful when a text is edited by several people.

➢ Select Track changes in one of the exercise texts on the Review tab.

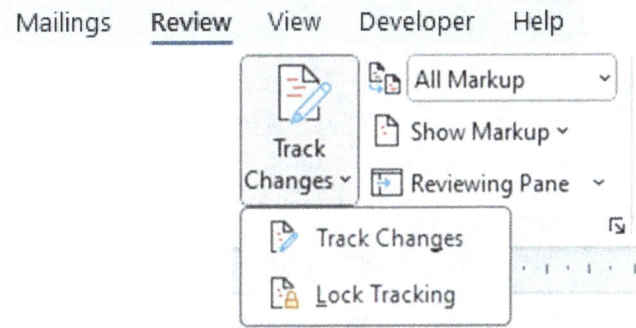

➢ With "Track changes" you enable changes to be marked, "Lock Tracking" prevents other users from deleting the tracking markings without the password entered here.

➢ Change a~~few~~some Words. All changes are now highlighted in color with deleted text only being crossed out:

➢ Change a~~few~~some Words. All changes are now highlighted in color with deleted text only being crossed out:

The options for marking mean:

♦ Markup (the type of marking):

   ↳ Simple Markup: Only a line in the right margin marks which places have been changed,

   ↳ All Markup: All modifications are displayed,

   ↳ No Markup: Changes are not marked,

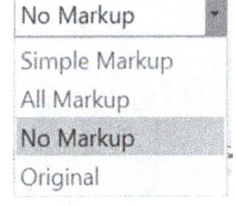

can also be used to turn off the markup function, because Word actually saves all changes, but they are usually not marked.

   ↳ Original: Show state before the corrections, don't worry, the last changes are not deleted, switch to one of the markup options and they will be displayed again.

♦ Show Markup: Here you can set which changes should be marked and whether they should be displayed in speech bubbles or directly in the text (inline).

♦ Reviewing Pane: Show a window in which the changes are displayed, either vertically next to the text or horizontally at the bottom. Click again to turn it off.

A decision is required after the correction process:

- You can press the right mouse button on any change and accept or reject it, or in the toolbar on Review:

All corrections can be accepted in the drop-down menu.

Forward, backward: go through the changes and accept or reject them individually.

Changes

- You can also simply save and close a text. Then the changes are saved in color and can be undone or checked later.

With "Accept all and stop tracking" you can stop to display corrections, also with "Reject all and stop tracking", but then you have lost all changes.

Accept Reject

8.6.1 Set Changes

Final note: you can use the expansion arrow in the Tracking menu to set what should be marked.

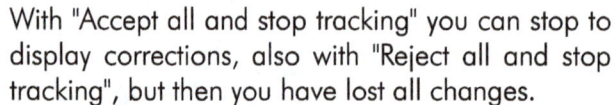

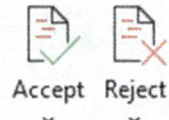

If you uncheck formatting there, for example, changes to text formatting, font and color, for example, will no longer be marked.

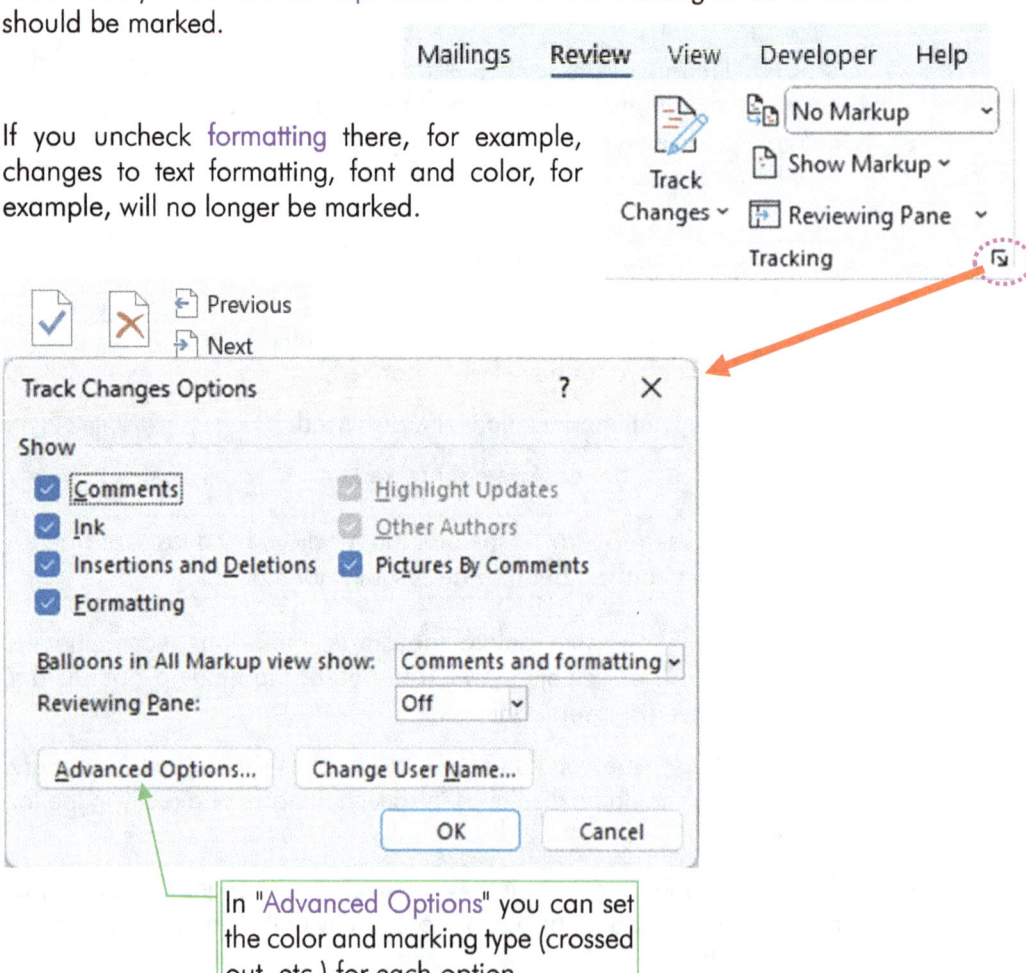

In "Advanced Options" you can set the color and marking type (crossed out, etc.) for each option.

Part Three

Graphics

in Word: drawing, inserting images, Photos, Tables...

9. Drawing in Word

In Word, we can paint simple pictures, but we can also insert photos and ClipArts into the text or use them as background. Let's start with Drawing.

9.1 The Symbols for Illustrations

These drawing symbols can be found in the Insert menu:

Pictures Shapes Icons 3D   SmartArt Chart Screenshot
                          Models

Illustrations

It means:

Pictures

- ♦ Pictures: insert a photo or a painted finished Picture (Graphic). In the selection menu you have three options:

  - ↳ This Device…: The Insert Picture menu will appear, where you can select a folder with photos or ClipArts from your drives.

  - ↳ Stock Images…: This has little to do with the archive, because selected images are displayed here as advertising to point out that all images are available to MS Office 365 users.

  - ↳ Online Pictures…: Insert a photo online from the Microsoft library, many categories can be selected, e.g., airplanes, cars, animals, ocean and much more.

> **Insert Picture From**
>
>  This Device…
>
>  Stock Images…
>
>  Online Pictures…

Shapes

- ♦ Shapes combine drawn elements such as arrows, stars, etc. A detailed description follows in the next chapter.

- ♦ Icons: Simplest black-and-white symbols, see examples in the margin.

- ♦ 3D Models: Rotatable three-dimensional bodies, such as dinosaurs, astronauts, etc.

  - ↳ This Device…: in your drives = still empty; or with "Stock 3D Models…" from a very extensive online MS collection.

- ♦ Insert Chart follows later since there are many setting options here.

- ♦ Screenshot: a screenshot can be taken from an opened window and inserted immediately into the current Word text.

9.2 Shapes and Drawing

There are numerous prefabricated graphic elements in Shapes:

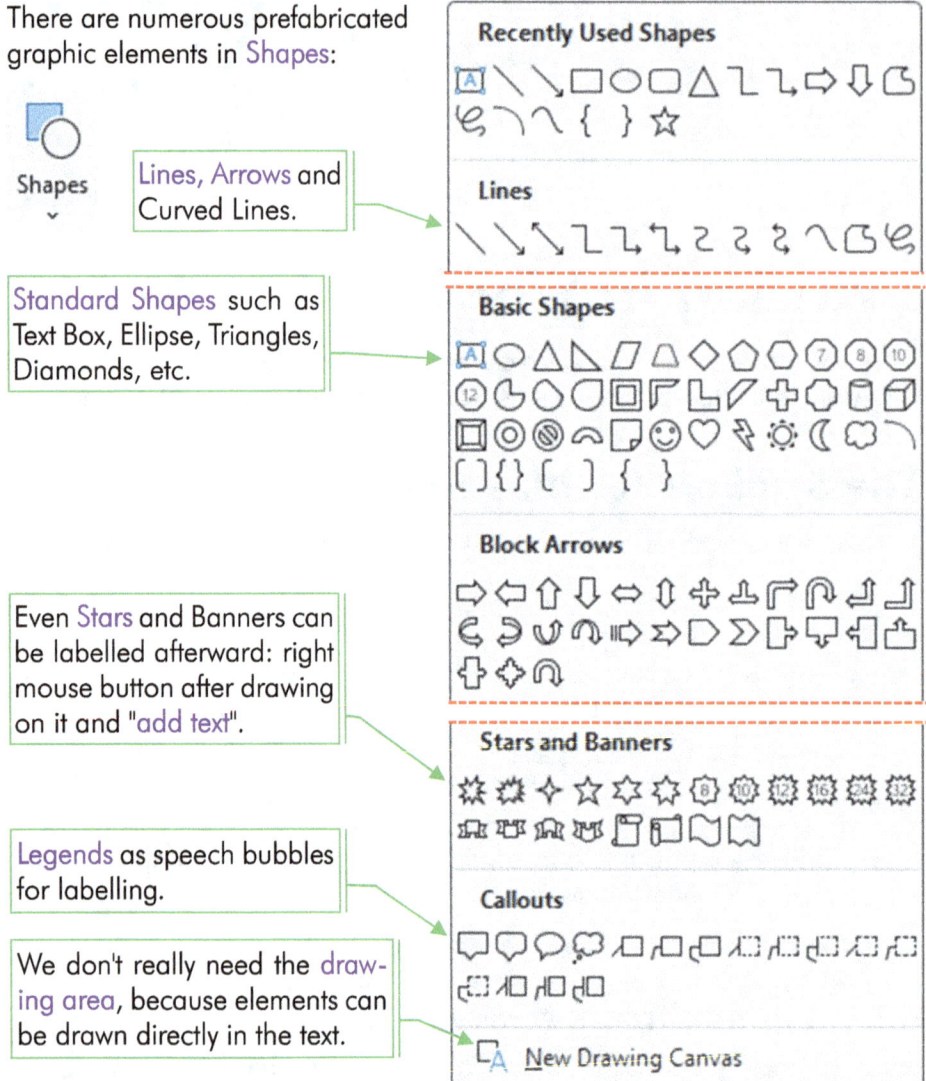

Lines, Arrows and Curved Lines.

Standard Shapes such as Text Box, Ellipse, Triangles, Diamonds, etc.

Even Stars and Banners can be labelled afterward: right mouse button after drawing on it and "add text".

Legends as speech bubbles for labelling.

We don't really need the drawing area, because elements can be drawn directly in the text.

➢ Insert a shape, such as an arrow, by selecting a shape and drawing with the mouse button pressed until the size fits.

✍ Then click at the handle points and move or resize.

The Draw commands appear when you click the shape and click "Shape Format" at the top of the Word bar:

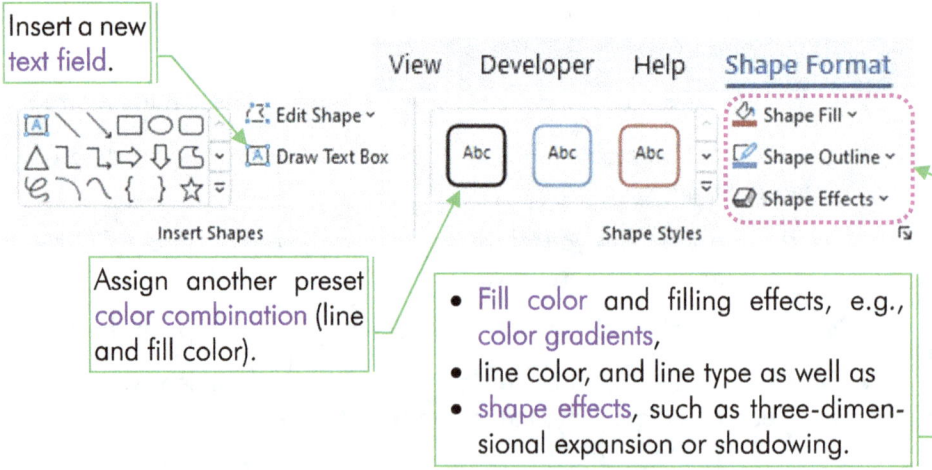

Insert a new text field.

Assign another preset color combination (line and fill color).

- Fill color and filling effects, e.g., color gradients,
- line color, and line type as well as
- shape effects, such as three-dimensional expansion or shadowing.

Note this:

- ◆ The symbols with arrows open submenus in which the selectable options are illustrated with further images.

- ◆ If you do not move the mouse over a symbol for a short time, the meaning will be displayed.

9.3 Wrapp Text

In order to be able to use graphics correctly in text, it is important to be able to set the text wrapping as desired.

- ◆ At Position, the arrangement on the sheet can be determined, e.g. right above or in the middle.

- ◆ By "Shape Format", you can set the order of the text wrapping, e.g., whether the graphic should be placed before or behind the text.

  - ↳ You can access the same setting options with the right mouse button when Wrap Text.

The options for text wrapping:

- ◆ In Line with Text: The graphic hangs like a letter in the text at the current cursor position. Can be used for small symbols.

- ◆ Square and Tight: Text flows around the graphic as in a newspaper, while Tight closely following the contours.

- ◆ Through is oddly like Tight.

  - ↳ Transparency could be set with "In Front of Text", then at top by "Shape Format" Drawing Tools Shape Fill/More fill Colors.

- ◆ Top and Bottom: the text will only resume after the graphic.

- ◆ Behind.../In Front of Text: the graphic can, for example, be placed behind the text like a watermark.

  - ↳ A text wrapping can also be created manually by indenting the paragraphs, which prevents annoying Word helplines.

- ◆ Edit Wrap Points: A frame around the image indicates where the text extends; this frame can be moved using the mouse at the handle points and thus adjusted.

The handle points of this text frame can be moved with the mouse to individually adjust the text flow

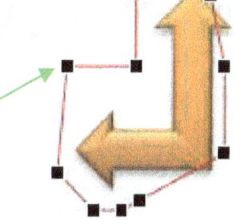

9.4 Drawing and AutoShapes

♦ Even if you click on a photo, you can also click on "Picture Format" at the top to display the commands which are slightly different from the commands for shapes, similar "Shape Format" for graphics:

"Picture Format" Tools for photos:

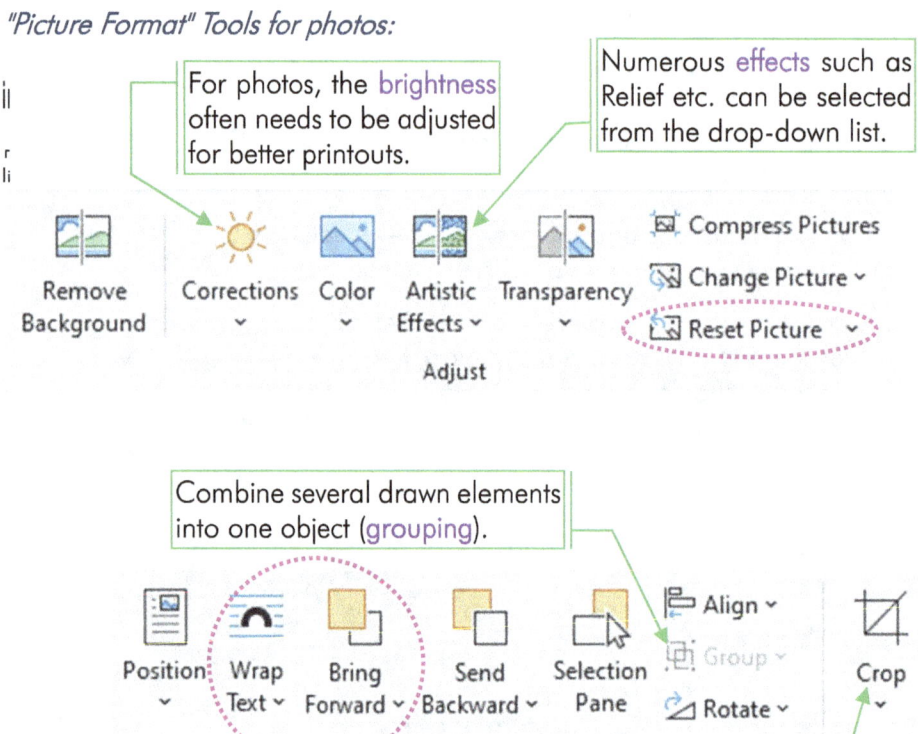

For photos, the brightness often needs to be adjusted for better printouts.

Numerous effects such as Relief etc. can be selected from the drop-down list.

Combine several drawn elements into one object (grouping).

Place selected elements in front of or behind the text or other drawings.

For example, you can trim edges of photos with Crop.

Difference photos and graphics:

"Picture Format" Tools for photos:	"Shape Format" for graphics:

Photos, usually scanned photos or already taken with a digital camera, consist of thousands of dots whose color is stored (pixels). In contrast to photos, graphics are drawn images, which means they are usually much simpler and have single-color areas instead of thousands of different color dots.

9.5 Resize, Move, and Delete

It doesn't matter what you draw: whether a line or a rectangle or an AutoShape, everything has to be first adjusted to the right size and moved to the right place.

♦ Always the same principle: select a shape, then draw in the text with the pressed mouse, click and adjust size and position.

Always applies to Edit:

♦ Click on the element to display the handle points.

↳ Now you can change the size at the handle points or

↳ Move on a line between the handle points or

↳ delete the selected part with [Delete].

Note the handle points, if they are visible, the frame will be highlighted and you can adjust or position the frame:

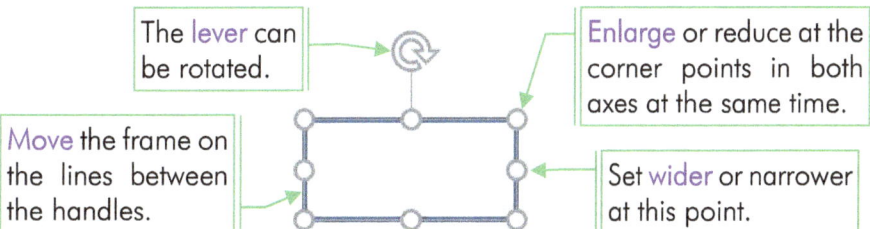

The lever can be rotated.

Enlarge or reduce at the corner points in both axes at the same time.

Move the frame on the lines between the handles.

Set wider or narrower at this point.

> Tip: By holding down the [Shift] key you can draw circles instead of ellipses, squares instead of rectangles and lines with exactly 0°, 30°, 45°, 60° or 90° degrees.

Try it out:

➤ Draw a line (keep the mouse button pressed).

➤ Extend the line.

➤ Rotate the line: move the handle points.

➤ Move the whole line (touch on the line).

➤ Change the line color to red.

➤ Select a 3pt bold dotted line.

➤ Delete the line.

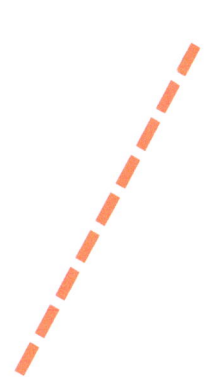

A Rectangle:

➤ Draw a rectangle and click on the new rectangle.

➤ Expand the rectangle to the right.

➤ Change the line color to blue and the fill color to yellow.

➤ Rotate: if you click on the rectangle or any other element, the handle points appear as well as a small lever where you can rotate the objects.

➤ Select a thin double line for the rectangle.

➤ Also, delete the rectangle again.

10. Insert Images

Now you want to insert a finished image (ClipArt). There are many ClipArts available online for MS Office that can be used in texts.

10.1 Exercise Preparing New Year's Eve

The drawing tools are described in the previous chapter starting on page 47.

➢ Start a new text again (empty document).

➢ First set the page format to DIN A5 for Layout/Format, 2cm for land-scape alignment and page margins (user-defined) everywhere.

➢ Use Return to create a few empty paragraphs (always good before formatting), then write the heading New Year's Eve Party at the top and format as shown (at startup),

✎ mark the text and stretch a bit: right mouse button/font/advanced card and spread apart by spacing at a distance of about 6pt.

✎ The filling can be set in the menu Home with the frame symbol:

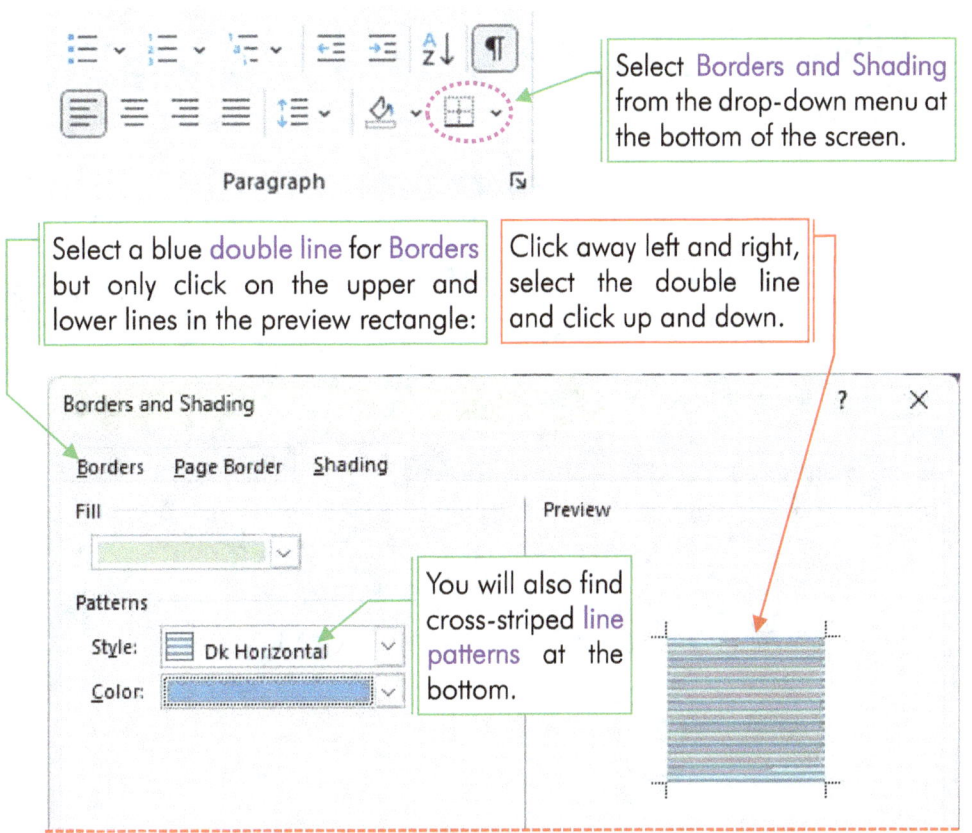

Select Borders and Shading from the drop-down menu at the bottom of the screen.

Select a blue double line for Borders but only click on the upper and lower lines in the preview rectangle:

Click away left and right, select the double line and click up and down.

You will also find cross-striped line patterns at the bottom.

10.2 Arrange text using a text box

➢ Arrange the rest of the text in two text fields and set line color and font:

   ↳ In the Insert menu, use the icon to insert a simple text box, then arrange and resize it.

   ↳ Text fields can be moved by keeping the mouse button pressed down on the frame lines and the size of the handle points can be changed.

   ↳ Setting the text box: Press the right mouse button on the margin line and select "Format Shape", then set by fill a color with 50% transparency as shown or disable the fill and line colors completely.

> When the first text field is finished, copy it, move it to the right and overwrite the text - there is no need to set it twice.

➢ Insert the Internet address as WordArt (see the first volume). The curved shape can be selected for drawing Shape Format/Text Effects/ABC Transform.

➢ Finally, insert ClipArts (description follows next page), position and vary the size of the text and ClipArts to fit the layout.

> You can also try the ready-made text boxes.

It should be something like this:

10.3 Insert ClipArt

These different possibilities exist (see p. 47):

- ♦ With Insert/Images/This Device: insert an image (photo, clip art). A window similar to Windows Explorer will appear to select the image file from your media.

Scanning
  - ✎ Scan images: first scan with the software of your scanner or a photo program and save as a photo, then load it into Word with the above command.

- ♦ Insert/Images/Online Images starts an MS Photo Gallery which displays sorted photos stored on the Internet in folders, e.g. airplanes, flowers, etc.

- ♦ Pictograms: small black and white icons, 3D models: a small selection of spatially drawn objects. SmartArt: for flowcharts.

- ➢ Select one or two 3D models from the Insert menu.

- ➢ Search the Internet for "ClipArt Party", download one or two and save them to your hard drive, then use Insert/Images/This Device to insert it into the document and arrange them.

The Page Background:

- ➢ To make it easier to arrange the Text Frames, press the right mouse button on a margin line, then select by "Wrap Text" "In front of text".

- ➢ You can add a page background to Design/Page Color/Fill Effects…, e.g. a default setting.

  - ✎ Take a look at the very nice graphics backgrounds on the Texture Index Card.

10.4 Edit Images

Word can do that too. Even finished ClipArts can be edited.

- ➢ On a clip art, press the right mouse button, then select "Edit Picture" or Group/Ungroup. Confirm the message "… to be converted" if necessary.

  - ✎ Grouping is only active if the ClipArt was drawn from multiple elements that were grouped.

Subsequently, you have all the commands at your disposal that you have already become acquainted with while drawing.

- ➢ Click on the desired one and change some colors: click on "Picture-, Graphics- or Shape Format" at the top, depending which element you have picked, where you can change the fill color with the color bucket.

You can also move, copy, delete, or resize objects. Obviously, selecting multiple objects can be difficult. Pay attention to the handle points when clicking.

> If you have seriously defaced the graphic, undo or delete it and reinsert it. Therefore, never edit the original image.

10.5 The Graphics Toolbar

A toolbar with many options appears when you select an inserted clip art or a photo click and select Image or drawing tools or image tools at the top, here as example for photos:

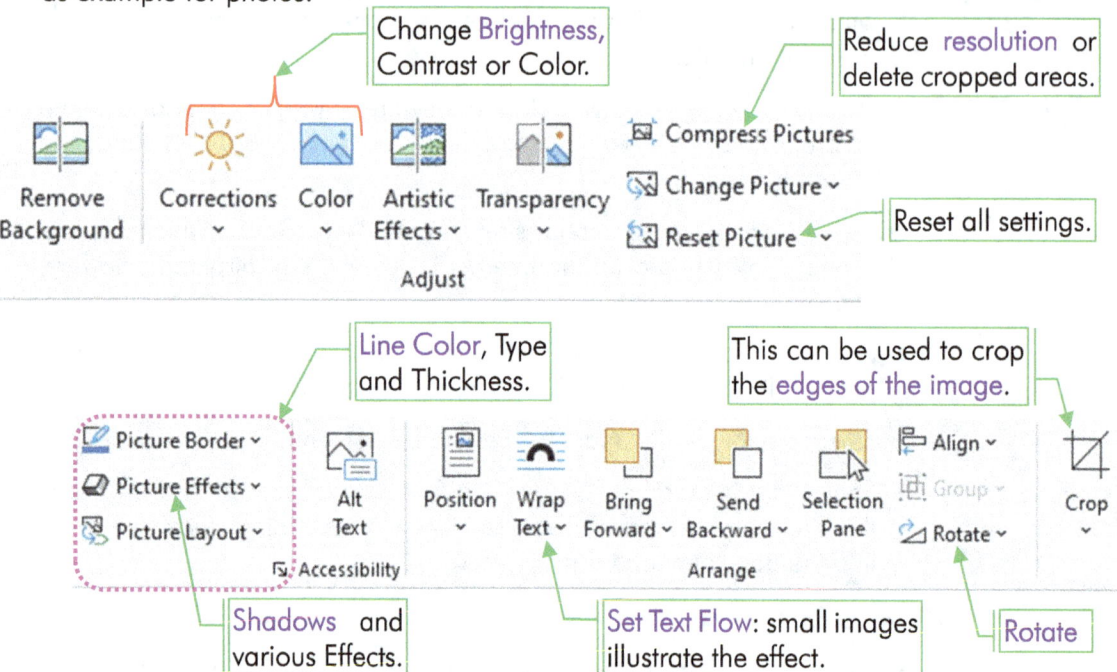

The Wrap Text (see p. 49) determines whether the text flows around the graphic as in a newspaper or whether the text continues in front of or behind the graphic, e.g. to use the graphic as a background.

(see p. 49)

You will find these interesting options under "Corections" and "Color":

- Brighter, darker or convert to black and white, see the preview images.

- Recolor: all Colors will be replaced by the selected Color.

- Set Transparent Color: You can use the eyedropper to click on a color that becomes hidden, i.e. transparent, as with "Remove Background", but here you can specify the color.

  ↳ This can be used, for example, to crop an unwanted monochrome background around an object.

  ↳ Works only for photos and only for one hue, not for color gradients such as a sky consisting of light and darker blue.

- Picture Color Options: the full menu opens, but some options are only available for photos while others are available for graphics.

> In case the line spacing is set to exact as well as text flow "with text in line", Word will only display this line height for the graphic while the rest of the image will be truncated. If necessary, do not set the line spacing to exact or change the text flow for the graphic.

- You can also use Windows Explorer to drag images from there to Word.

Optimal for Word is wmf-Vector files or Images in jpg or png format. Here it is helpful if the file extensions are visible.

11. Letter with Graphic Elements

Not all letters are the same. A few simple lines transform the letter into a design. The letterhead, which, if the text is two or more pages long, should be repeated on each new page should be placed in the header line. An illustration can be found after the description.

11.1 The Header

As already mentioned, the letterhead is placed in the header, because what is entered in the header or footer is automatically repeated on each page.

The Header or Footer:

Header

Close Header and Footer

- ◆ Only the first time in the Insert menu activates Header, then double-click the header or footer to open it,

  - ☝ to exit from the toolbar ... press "Close..." or simply double-click in the text area.

- ◆ Layout/Margins/Custom Margins defined on the Layout tab can be used to set the spacing of the header or footer to the paper margin. The actual size of the header or footer depends on the text entered.

For Exercise:

- ➤ Insert/Header/Blank takes you to the header.

  - ☝ You will already find some predefined header lines in the Header dropdown list. For practice, however, we will set up our first header manually, after which you will easily understand the predefined headers.

WordArt

- ➤ Create the company logo on the Insert with WordArt file card, write the address with small caps and special characters centered below it.

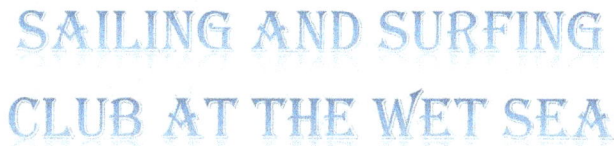

SAILING AND SURFING CLUB AT THE WET SEA

Beach Street 56 ✦ 519 Wet Water
☎567 / 567 567 📱 567 / 567 567 5

- ➤ Close the header and set the address repetition to very small 8pt font size.

  SAILING AND SURFING CLUB AT THE WET SEA
  Beach Street 56 ✦ 519 Wet Water

- ➤ Draw the line (insert/shapes) for demarcation.

11.2 Arrange the drawing parts firmly

Draw a short thin, dotted line in the left margin as a folding aid. This line should not move with the text and should be positioned exactly at 10 cm:

➤ Click on the line and enter 10 cm from the page for the vertical position under Shape Format/Position/More layout options.

↳ This automatically disables "Move object with text" so that the lines no longer move with the text.

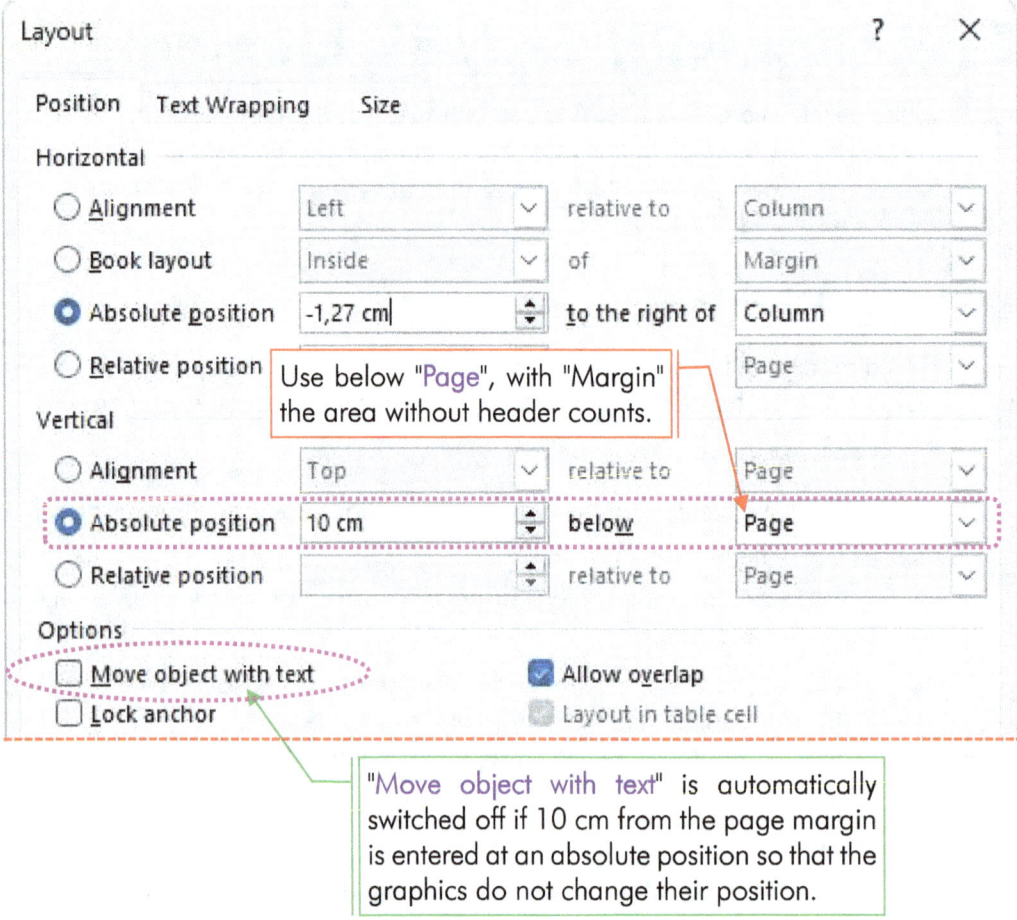

➤ Copy this line and arrange the copy at 20cm.

♦ Move object with text: the ClipArt hangs with an anchor at the paragraph in front and moves with it.

♦ This paragraph is permanently assigned to the anchor by fixing it. The anchor stays with this paragraph even if you move the image.

↳ Only required for problem cases, e.g. multi-column text.

↳ If you want to anchor firmly, you should set the drawing anchors visibly, which is possible with File/Options on the Display tab:

11.3 Image as Watermark

Now we add an Image as a Watermark.

- ♦ We could do this with Design/Watermark/Custom Watermark or Design/Page Color/Fill Effects/Picture but both methods are difficult to arrange as page backgrounds.

- ➢ Insert a sailboat: on the Insert tab, choose Pictures/Online Pictures, then enter by "Search for:" sailing and confirm with Return or OK.

Set Image as Watermark:

- ➢ Assign an image style sheet to the photo: Drawing Tools/Format:

- ➢ Reduce the image, move it to the lower right corner and try an artistic effect that brightens the photo like a watermark:

- ➢ Do not forget to save! The letter will be used again later.

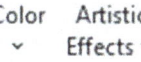

Color   Artistic
  ˅   Effects ˅

SAILING AND SURFING CLUB
AT THE WET SEA

Beach Street 56 ✦ 519 Wet Water
☎ 567 / 567 567   📄 567 / 567 567 5

SAILING AND SURFING CLUB AT THE WET SEA
Beach Street. 56 ➲ 519 Wet Water

«firstname» «name»
«number» «street»
«district»
«city» «postcode»

> The placeholders for the address are appropriately overwritten for each letter or as in Chapter 16 described is automatically filled out using the mail merge function.

Ladies and Gentlemen,

> A gap for the text. Don't forget to save the letter under a new filename with "Save as" right before filling it in.

With kind regards

> The footer is separated from the rest of the letter by a blue line.

Board of Directors:
Dr. Muller-Duck
John Michel Waterblue

Bank details:
WaveMoneyGroup, BIC GBW848e7
IBAN US 595 954 526 599 759 457 945 97

12. A Presentation

The Style sheets may be used in this chapter. We will also create columns, insert a header, images, and tables. You will find the finished exercise as a template at the end of this chapter.

12.1 Create Columns

First, we to set the page format.

➤ Open the Sugar[3] Exercise Text.

➤ Set up the page on the Layout tab: Landscape format and 3cm page margin at the top, because this is where the heading is placed in the header, otherwise reduce the page margins to 1cm (user-defined).

Now the three columns are missing:

➤ For columns, you could set the default to 3 columns, but in the following "More columns" menu, you can set the spacing between columns.

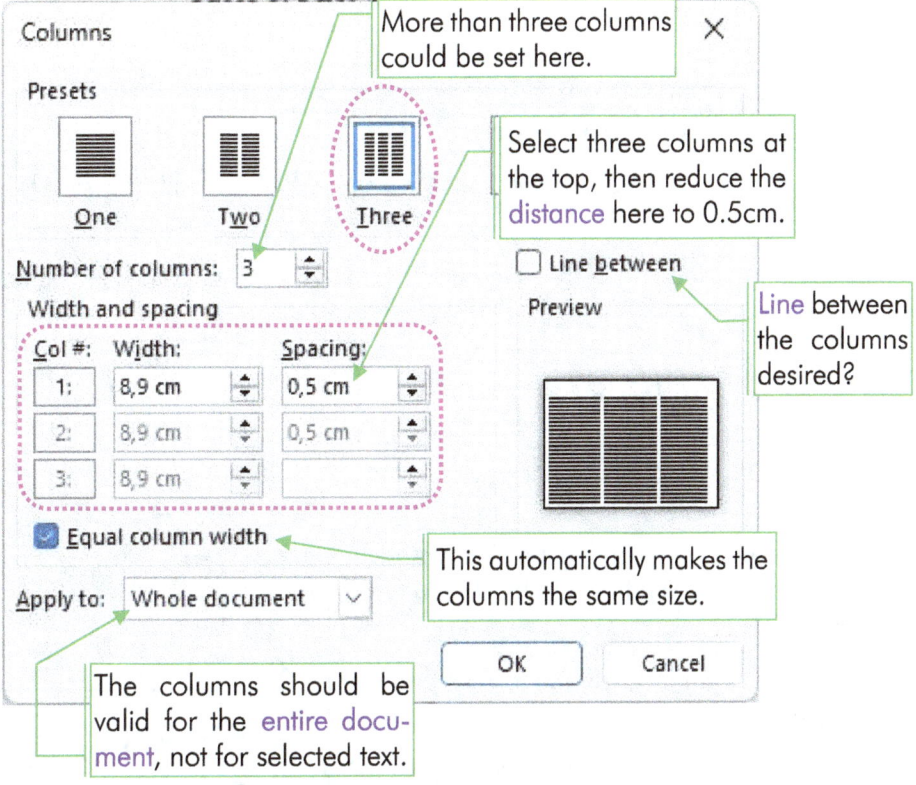

_____

3 This Sugar text is a slightly modified sample text from one of the first versions of MS Word.

> If only one paragraph is to be set with several columns: Mark the paragraph and choose "Apply to: Marked text".

➢ Save the exercise with File/Save As in your exercise folder so that the original file is not overwritten.

    ↳ When saving as a file type, select "Word document" (at the top of the drop-down list) to save in the current Word format.

12.2 Formatting with Style Sheets

Now you have three equal columns. The unformatted text quickly becomes a print-ready document with style sheets. Most texts contain the following text blocks:

> Title page, opening credits, table of contents
> Headings: Heading 1 Heading 2...
> normal Text: Text body and Standard
> special Text: Bullet, Enumeration
> End of Text: Appendix, references, etc.

The title can be set without a style sheet, as this is an isolated case.

➢ Assign Heading 1 to the main headings and Heading 2 to the table headings.

> The shortcuts [Alt]-1, 2 and 3 are already set up for the style sheets Heading 1, 2 and 3. Save work by using these shortcuts. If not defined, you should set this up in the Styles menu under Format/Shortcut for Headings 1 to 3, see next chapter.

[Alt]-1, 2, 3

12.2.1 Set style sheets via the menu

There are several ways to change the style sheet. We start with the simplest one.

➢ Click on a Heading 1, then Heading 1 is marked in the Style sheet menu:

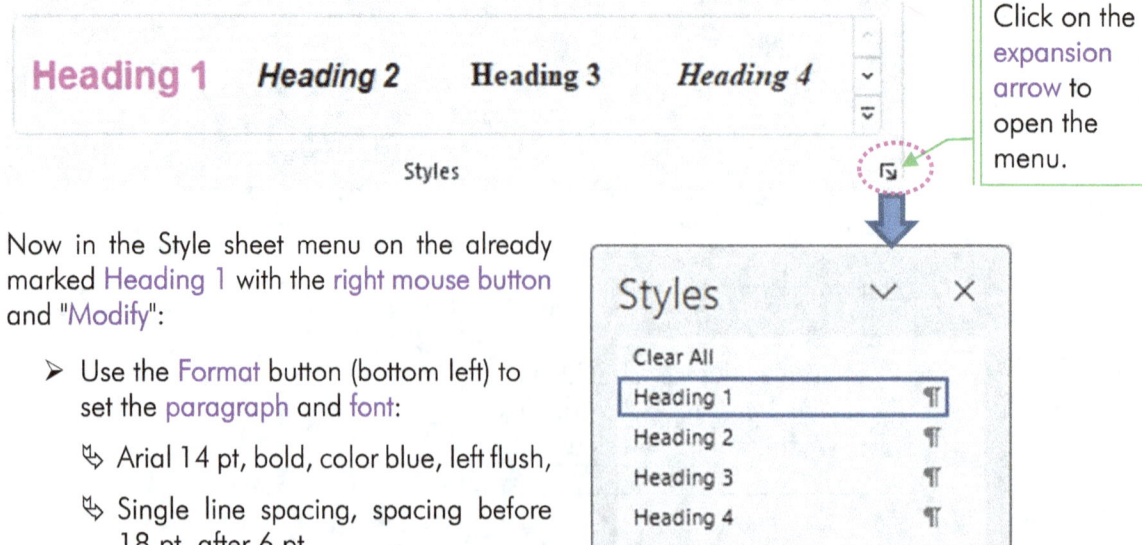

Click on the expansion arrow to open the menu.

Now in the Style sheet menu on the already marked Heading 1 with the right mouse button and "Modify":

➢ Use the Format button (bottom left) to set the paragraph and font:

    ↳ Arial 14 pt, bold, color blue, left flush,

    ↳ Single line spacing, spacing before 18 pt, after 6 pt.

The Sub-Heading:

➢ Format Heading 2 for the table headings as follows: "is based on: " Change heading 1, font size to 12pt, pre-spacing to 6pt.

You will find it in the style menu above:

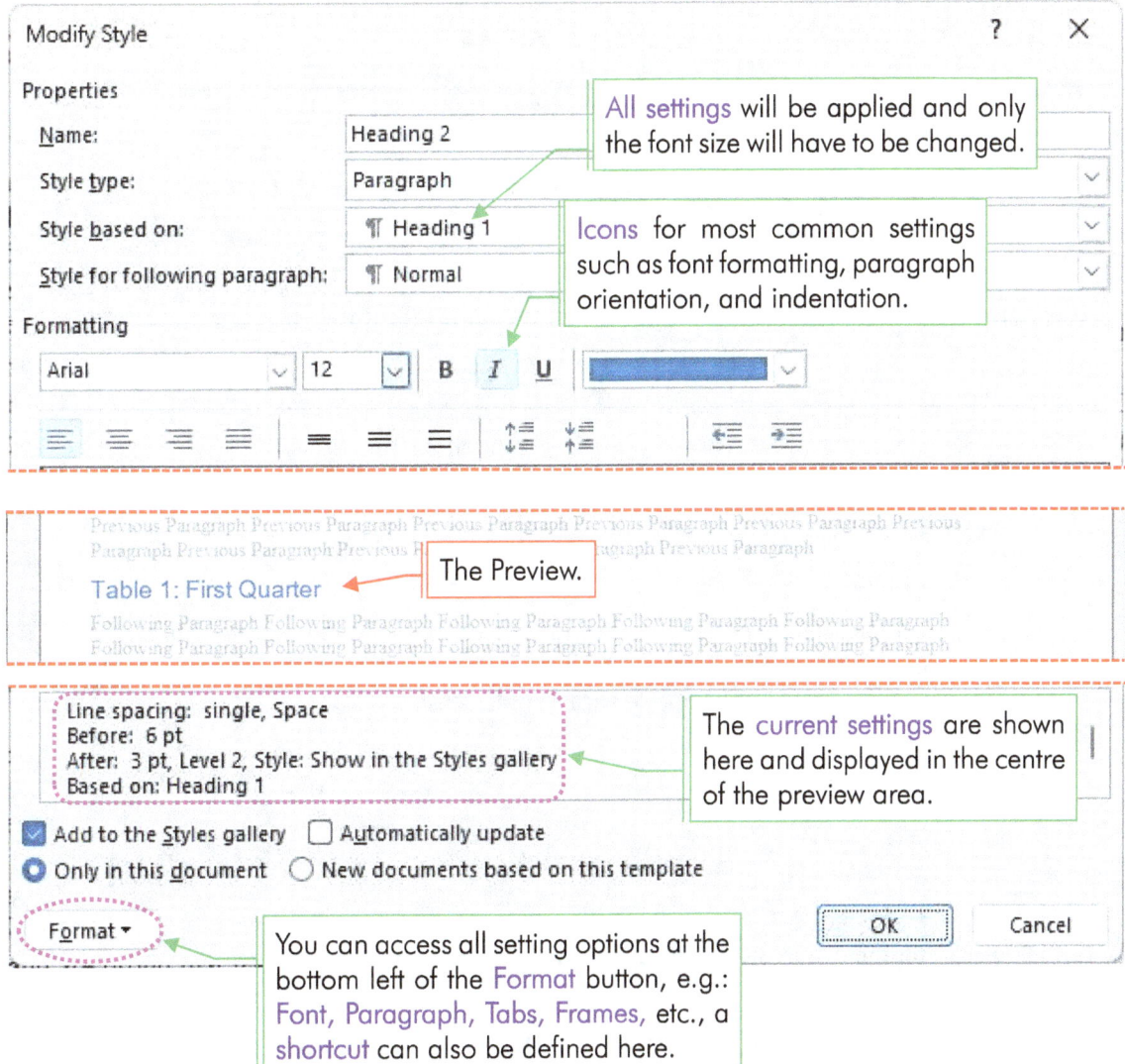

12.2.2 Update Style Sheet

There is another convenient way to apply settings to the style sheet.

➢ Select the first text block completely e.g. by clicking three times fast and set for the normal text:

   ✍ Arial font with 12pt font size, justification, simple line spacing.

➢ Now click the right mouse button on the normal style in the Style menu and select "Update normal to match selection".

➢ Check whether hyphenation is activated so that the lines are not drawn too far apart by the justification (Layout/Hyphenation/Automatic).

12.2.3 Create a new Style Sheet

Almost every text requires the following style sheets: Standard, heading 1, 2, 3 and one or two special paragraphs, e.g. hanging or quotation.

> ➤ Create the style sheet "Bullet" with the bullet character for the paragraphs under "Highlights/Main Sequences" and "Perspectives":

> ✎ Choose a nice Bullet character, additionally based on standard,
> ✎ spacing before and after each 3 pt.
> ✎ indented by 0.5 cm and suspended by 0.5 cm instead of the default setting of 0.63:

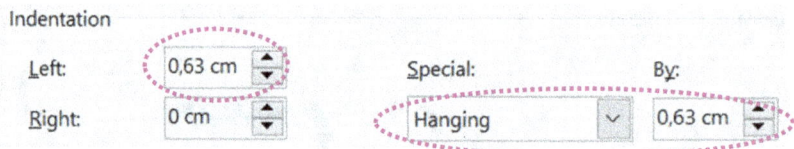

> ✎ Enter Bullet as the name of the style sheet.

12.2.4 Assign a new Style Sheet

> ➤ Now assign Bullet to the other paragraphs as well.

> ✎ You can either click on a paragraph or highlight paragraphs and select a style sheet in the Style sheet quick selection or use the expansion arrow to display the format template list:

> ◆ Highlighting related paragraphs only requires you to change to Bullet once.

> ✎ Note: the paragraphs do not have to be fully highlighted.

At the end of this chapter, you will find an illustration of the finished exercise, from which you can also learn which paragraphs should be formatted with particular style sheets.

12.3 The Table

Now it's time for the first table. The text is only separated by Tabulators.

This is a common Phenomenon:

> ◆ If, for example, you want to create a brochure from ten papers from a conference, some tables with tabs are set,

> ◆ or when data is transferred from other programs, the columns are often replaced by separators (tabs, semicolons, commas) between the columns.

12.3.1 Convert text to Table

No problem about Word, because we can convert text into a table and vice versa.

➢ Select the text according to Table 1 that belongs in the table.

➢ On the Insert tab, choose by Table "Convert Text to Table":

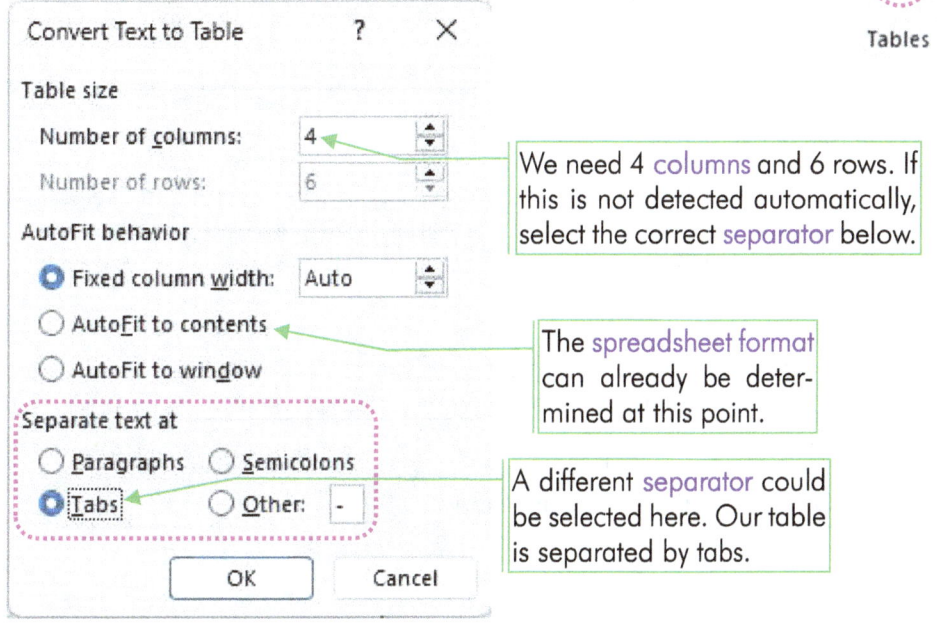

We need 4 columns and 6 rows. If this is not detected automatically, select the correct separator below.

The spreadsheet format can already be determined at this point.

A different separator could be selected here. Our table is separated by tabs.

If a table has been selected then you will find the return path: Convert table to text in the Table menu.

12.3.2 Set a Table

Now the table is formatted:

Click on this icon to select the entire table, right mouse button/table properties and centre cell vertically.

Select this line. Right click on it to connect cells with "Merge Cells" and it becomes a large cell.

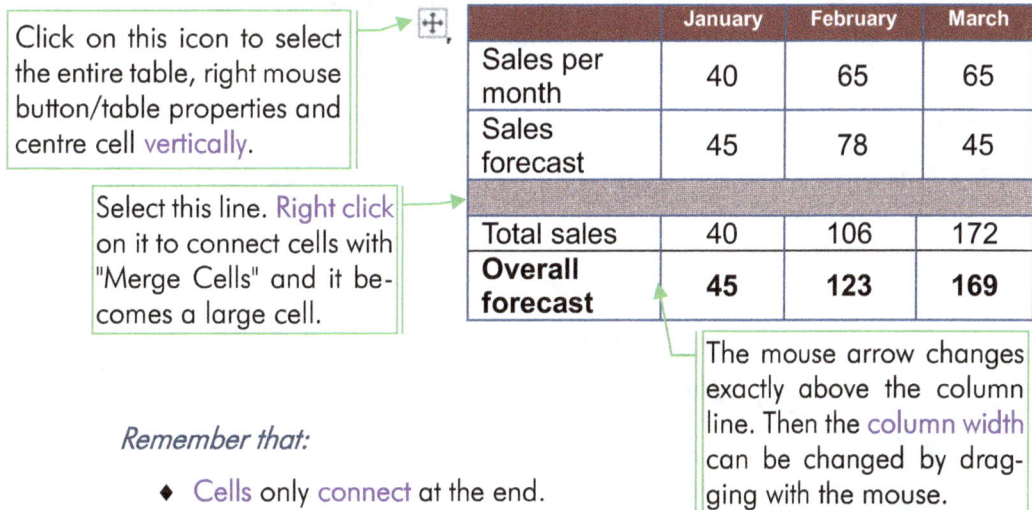

	January	February	March
Sales per month	40	65	65
Sales forecast	45	78	45
Total sales	40	106	172
Overall forecast	**45**	**123**	**169**

The mouse arrow changes exactly above the column line. Then the column width can be changed by dragging with the mouse.

Remember that:

◆ Cells only connect at the end.

◆ If you want to adjust something, first mark the right one.

    ✍ With the right mouse button on the marked area, e.g. on a marked column, the appropriate commands usually appear.

So the right mouse button often saves the search for the right command.

12.3.3 Filling and Lines

All filling settings are combined for "Borders and Shading", but some interesting settings can also be found directly in the Table Design and Layout Tabs, e.g., the Table Styles:

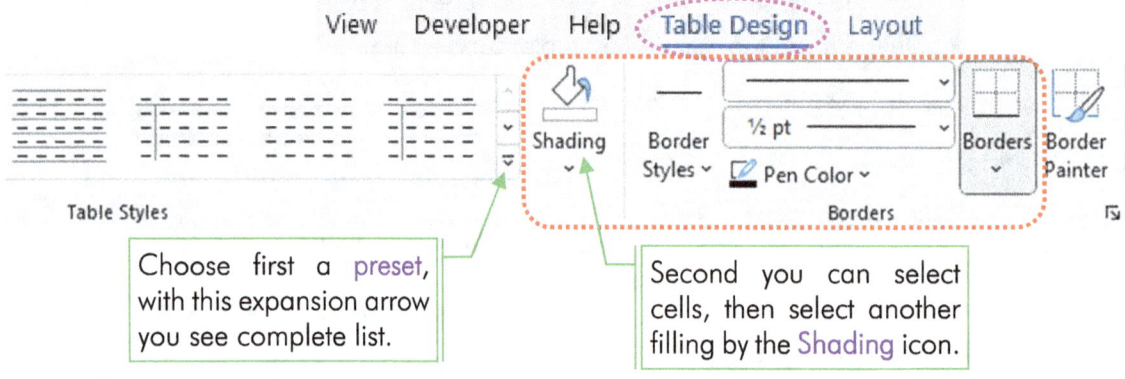

Choose first a preset, with this expansion arrow you see complete list.

Second you can select cells, then select another filling by the Shading icon.

Practical:

♦ You can set each row or column individually with the Table Tools, Table Properties, or as normal text at Home, e.g. for the font and font size.

> Check with test printouts, because especially with fillings the printout often looks different than indicated on the screen.

12.4 Insert Diagram

➢ With Insert/Pictures you can insert the file Sales Graphic into the texts of the exercises.

   ↳ Of course, you can set the cursor to the desired insertion position beforehand.

➢ Right mouse button on the graphic and you can select by "Wrap Text" "In line with text" or in front or behind the text, then create the free space for the graphic using empty paragraph marks.

Now the text in the first two columns must be adjusted:

➢ Change the font size, line spacing and paragraph spacing (only in the respective style sheet!) until the layout is the same as on the style sheet.

Revised Table of Market Positions

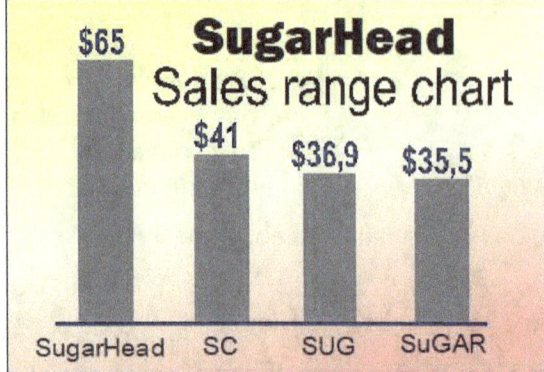

12.4.1 The Company Logo

consists of a ClipArt (= the frame) and the text that is placed in a text field to move it to the center of the frame.

> ➢ Choose: Insert/Pictures to insert the image *plaket1.wmf*, also to be found in the texts of the exercises.

> ➢ Move the image to the correct position at the end of the text and widen the still round image to the oval frame shown.

Complete the Text:

> ➢ Drag a text box (Insert/Text Box/Simple Text Box) and type in *SugarHead Ltd.*, set text size, and color.

Text Box ˅

> ➢ Then press the right mouse button on the text field and select Format Shape, especially hide the filling and line of the text field with "Line color: No line".

12.5 The Header Line

> ➢ The header is activated the first time in the Insert with Header-Menu. Select a suitable preset or an empty header.

> ➢ Write *SugarHead Ltd.* in the header line and adjust the font size accordingly, as well as lock the text wide (5 pt) and change the text color.

> ➢ Select a fill color from the Fill Bucket icon to color the background, matching to the font color.

> ➢ All done? Then close the Header, either with the icon or by double-clicking: double-click on the text area closes the header, double-click on the header opens it again.

Close Header and Footer

12.6 Headings at the beginning of a column

Word is preset so that the space before a paragraph is not inserted after a section or column change but at the first heading.

The simplest remedy: turn off the space in front of the first heading.

SugarHead Ltd.

Highlights/Main Sequences

✓ In march our sales have been higher as calculated, reach a level of a new sales record! This exceptional good result has been reached instead our shop advertisement and the very good work our sales representatives.

✓ At march 5th: The new sales strategy and product planning would discuss with the board of directors. A report of this meeting you could be request from Paul Brach.

✓ Through mailing of a special spring prospectus could be increased the regional sales about 50%.

Table 1: First Quarter

Sales forecast	January	February	March
Sales per month	40,982	65,832	65,929
Sales forecast	45,200	78,300	45,900
Total sales	40,982	106,814	172,743
Overall forecast	45,200	123,500	169,400

Business Report

Equal the sales of this march reflect the trend to increase of sales in this quarter. First time this year we have reached more sales as calculated.

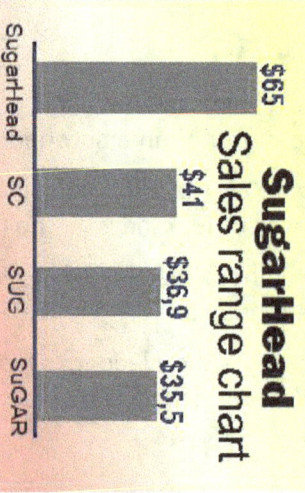

Revised Table of Market Positions

SugarHead
Sales range chart

Table 2: Second Quarter

Sales per Region	
Region 1	306
Region 2	312
Region 3	115
Region 4	235

Perspectives

✓ As result of the increased sales in last month specially in region 4 and the exceptions for the future for our company SugarHead Chocolates, we except for this whole year a sales volume of 1,000 units per month.

✓ With this level in future our company SugarHead Chocolates have reached the first position in the sales.

✓ As result of the increased sales in last month specially in region 4 and the exceptions for the future for our company SugarHead Chocolates, we except for this whole year a sales volume of 1,000 units per month.

✓ The sales increase of other companies in this business field will reach only less than half of our calculated increase. We have got for some minutes the final sales report and are proud that we can publish, that we have received this year a total sales record.

SugarHead Ltd.

Part Four

Table of Contents

A Table of Contents, Header, Page Numbers, a Section Break

13. A Table of Contents

Word can create a table of contents automatically and format it in an appealing way - a big relief, especially because the table of contents can be updated automatically after every change.

13.1 Format Text

This exercise is not ready either, but you should format the text first.

➢ Open the exercise text TableOfContent.doc and save it into the exercise folder.

➢ Go through the text and assign the style sheets Heading 1, 2 and 3 as indicated with the shortcuts or with the style menu.

♦ Use the shortcuts that are already set up for the headings:

↳ Heading 1 with [Alt]-1,

↳ Heading 2 with [Alt]-2,

↳ Heading 3 with [Alt]-3,

These Shortcuts are not on every keyboards available. If don't work, you open the style menu with the little arrwo by Home/Styles and use this menu.

Set the headings as follows:

➢ Heading 1 *:*

  ➢ Arial font with 20 pt font size, bold,
  ➢ Spacing before 30 pt, after 12 pt, line down with 3 pt spacing,
  ➢ Text and line color dark blue.

➢ Heading 2: based on Heading 1,

  ➢ but without a line and with only 16 pt font size,
  ➢ Spacing forward: 18 pt, after 6 pt.

➢ Heading 3: based on Heading 2,

  ➢ 14 pt, bold + italic, spacing before 12 pt, after 4 pt.

> Note: set in the style sheets of course!

13.2 Search and Replace

You will surely have noticed that the headings are misspelled. Not a writing error, but a frequent conversion error, because the text was taken over from another program.

➣ You could choose Home/Replace, but we would like to have a look at the search window: Home/Find or [Ctrl]-F:

🔍 Find ⌄

↻ᵇ꜀ Replace

⬈ Select ⌄

Editing

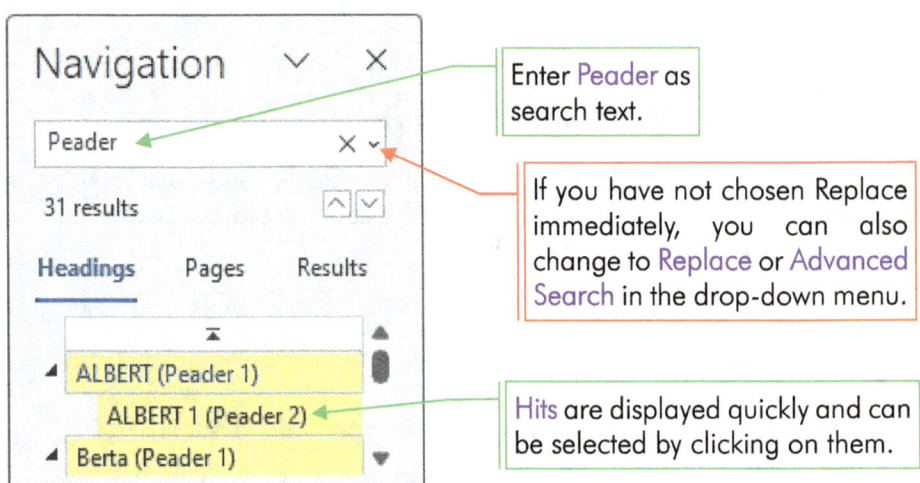

Enter Peader as search text.

If you have not chosen Replace immediately, you can also change to Replace or Advanced Search in the drop-down menu.

Hits are displayed quickly and can be selected by clicking on them.

➣ One of the ways to continue replacing. Specify the correct word "Heading" when replace with:

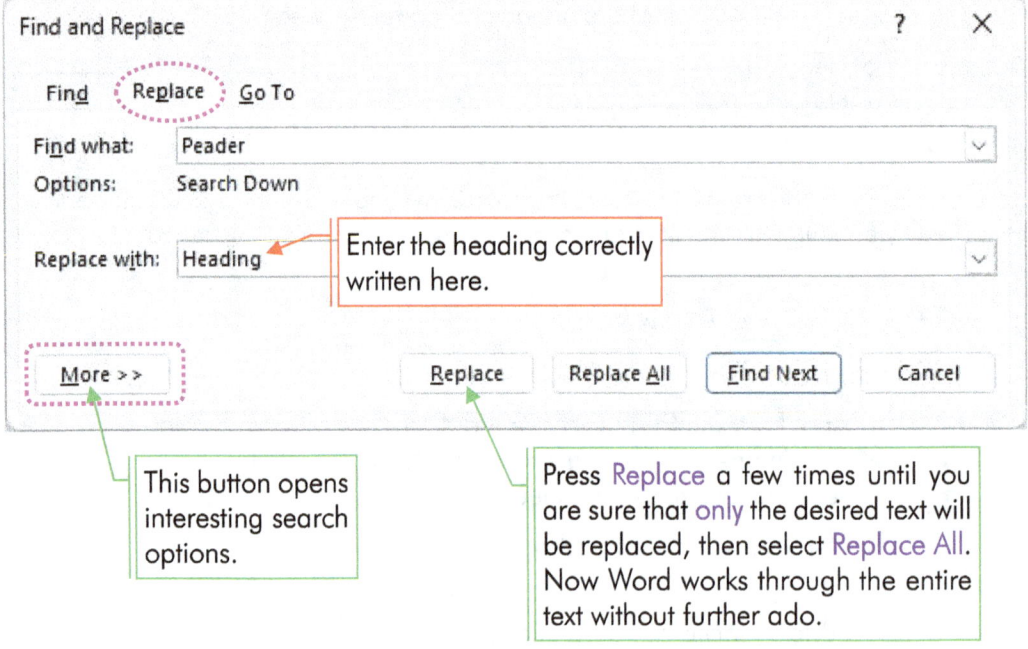

Enter the heading correctly written here.

This button opens interesting search options.

Press Replace a few times until you are sure that only the desired text will be replaced, then select Replace All. Now Word works through the entire text without further ado.

◆ If you find another error during replacement, you can correct it directly:

☶ click on the text twice with the mouse to correct the error.

☶ Then click on the Search window that is still open and continue the search, possibly only with Search: downwards.

The further refined possibilities of having something replaced are presented in the third volume.

13.3 Create a Table of Contents

In preparation, we insert a blank page after the title page on which the table of contents is to be inserted.

➢ Go to the end of the title page. Insert a few empty paragraph marks and press [Ctrl]-[Return] to insert an additional page break, so that there is now an empty second page.

➢ Simply write "Table of Contents" as the heading at the top of this page, highlight it and set it to 20 pt and bold – manually without using a format template.

✎ Because this heading "Table of contents" is not to be included in the table of contents, you may not use the style sheet heading under any circumstances.

Table of Contents ⌄

Generate the Directory:

➢ Now place the cursor under the heading on this empty page and select Table of Contents on the References card.

➢ You can select a preset from the drop-down menu or open the following settings menu with "Custom Table of Contents":

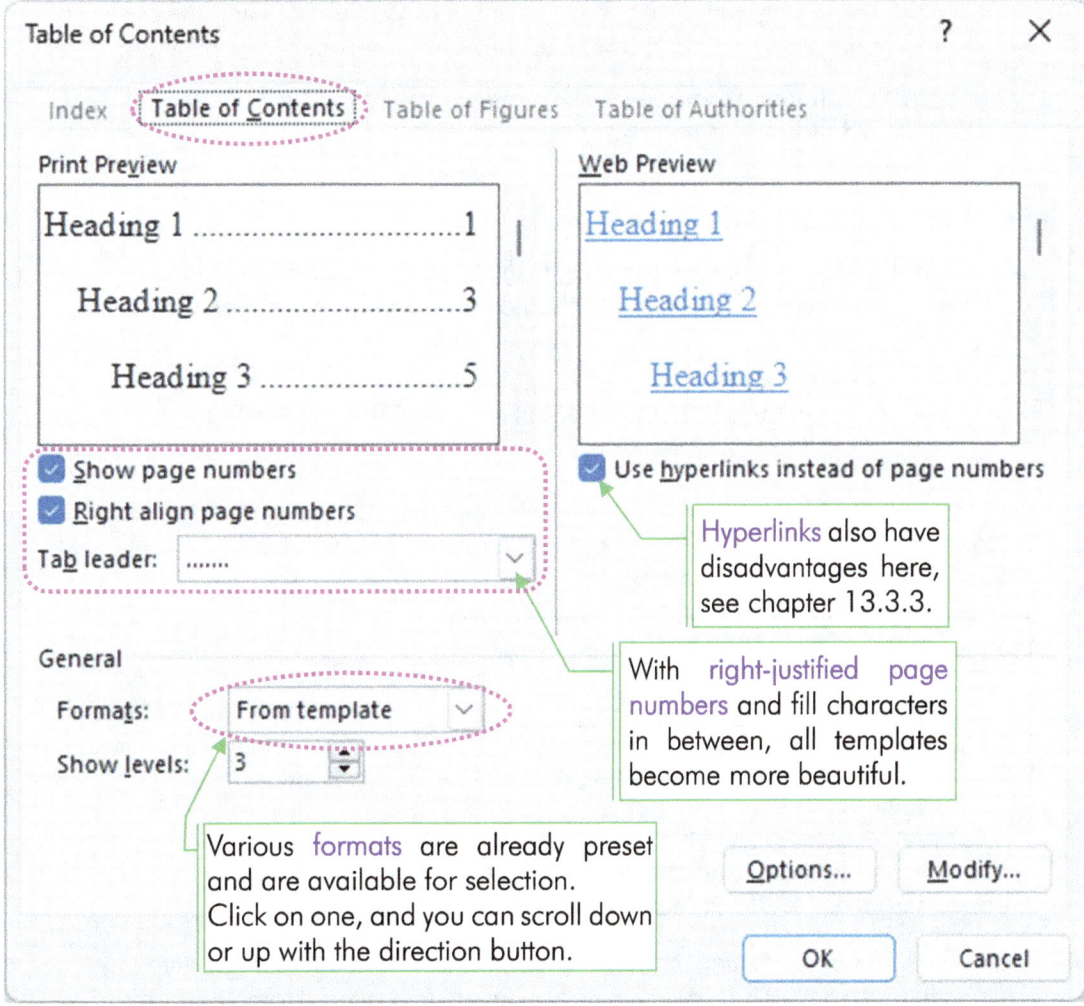

➢ Select a preset for "Formats" and start the action with OK.

13.3.1 Update Table of Contents

You can update the table of contents or regenerate the table of contents if you have changed the headings in the text:

The most practical option:

➢ Press the right mouse button over the table of contents, then select Update fields.

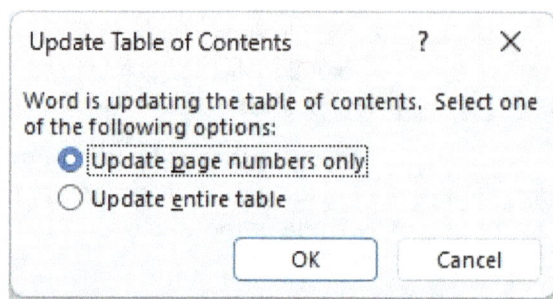

ᗰ You will then be asked if you only want to update the page numbers (e.g., if you change the font size).

ᗰ or update the entire directory, which is necessary if you have added, renamed or deleted new chapters.

You can perform the following operation from any text position because Word searches for the existing table of contents:

➢ Insert a new table of contents and confirm the appearing question "Replaced this table of content?"

ᗰ But works only with same "Custom Table of Contents", using the automatic tables will insert a second new one at actual cursor position.

ᗰ With "Formats: From Template", see previous page, the formatting of the old directory is retained.

13.3.2 Format Table of Contents

When Word creates a table of contents, it searches the text for the Headings 1, 2, and 3 style sheets. These texts are copied and assembled at the beginning of the text.

> A table of contents can therefore only be created automatically if the headings styles have been used!

Now the headings in the table of contents should not be printed with a font as large and bold as in the text. Therefore the style sheets for the table of contents are replaced according to this scheme:

Style sheets in Text	Styles in Table of Contents
Heading 1	TOC 1
Heading 2	TOC 2
Heading 3	TOC 3

You see in the styles menu if you mark a complete table of contents line.

This allows the table of contents to be formatted independently of the rest of the text using these "TOC" style sheets.

➢ Try this out by setting the style sheet TOC 1 differently, e.g., with a different font color: open the style sheet menu on Home with the expansion arrow and right click/change on directory 1.

13.3.3 To the "Hyperlink" style sheet

Hyperlink

- ♦ Hyperlinks you know from the Internet are like cross-references.

  ↳ You can jump to another position or page by clicking on it.

- ♦ This has the advantage that you can jump to the heading in the text by holding down the [Ctrl] key and clicking on the heading in the table of contents.

Problems with the table of contents because of the Hyperlink style sheet:

- ♦ The Hyperlink style is initially selected when you click on it. To still be able to set the style TOC, these methods are available:

  ↳ Click in the table of contents left in the margin to select a table of contents line, then the correct style TOC is displayed.

  ↳ Or manually change the desired style sheet in TOC 1, 2, etc. using the style menu.

  ↳ Or do without the "use hyperlinks instead of page numbers" function in the table of contents from the outset, see p. 73.

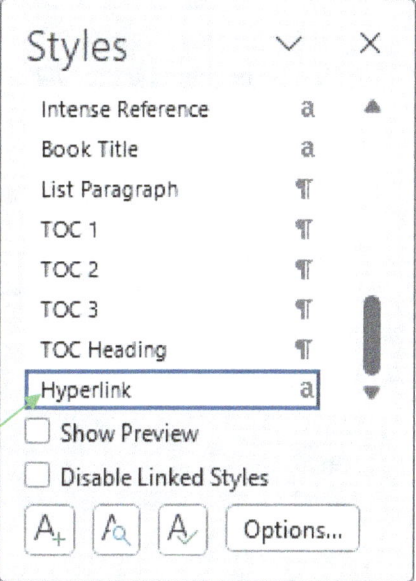

With "Hyperlinks" the actual style template "TOC" for Table of Contents is not selected, although clicked in the directory.

For practice the headings 1 in the table of contents should be inverted (white text on a black background):

- ➢ Set TOC 1 in the style sheet: shading of 100% blue. With text color Auto, the text automatically turns white, but only with 100% background fill. If not work with automatic color, switch the text color to white.

  ↳ 100% filling for laser printers, on inkjet printers a shading of 60 to 70% is recommended. For shaded values, text color white instead of the auto is required. Try it out.

Since the "Automatically update" option is selected in the directory style sheets, we can also change a paragraph manually; these changes are automatically adopted in the style sheet.

- ➢ Indent a paragraph on the right side of the ruler:

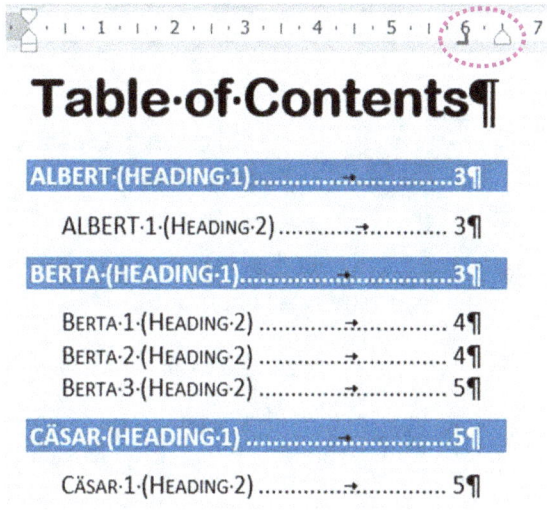

13.4 Numbering of Headings

Probably the page numbers are entered in your table of contents, but the numbering of the headings is still missing.

The numbering of the headings is not set in the table of contents, but in the text in the style sheets "Heading" and then transferred to the table of contents at the next update.

Click a heading 1 in the text, then this icon "list" and choose bottom in the drop-down list "Define new multilevel list".

This menu will appear, first press the "More" button at the bottom left so that the Style sheet button will be displayed:

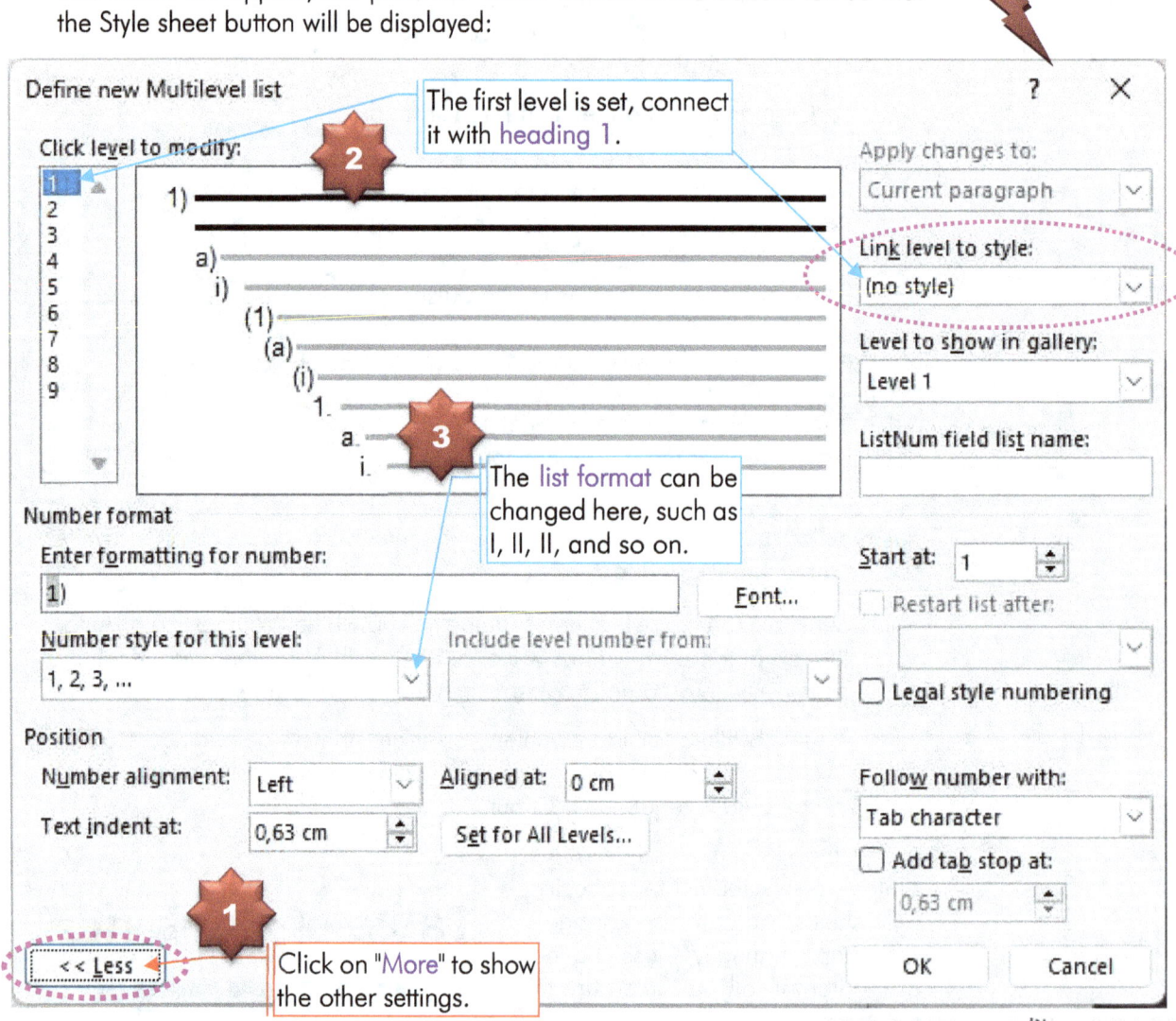

➢ Then set the distance between the number and the heading in the ruler appropriately.

Numbering in the Table of Contents:

➢ Once you have set the numbering, you can update the table of contents (Update entire directory) to include the numbers in the table of contents.

Continue to the second level:

> ➢ Click on left 2, connect right with heading 2 and level 2.

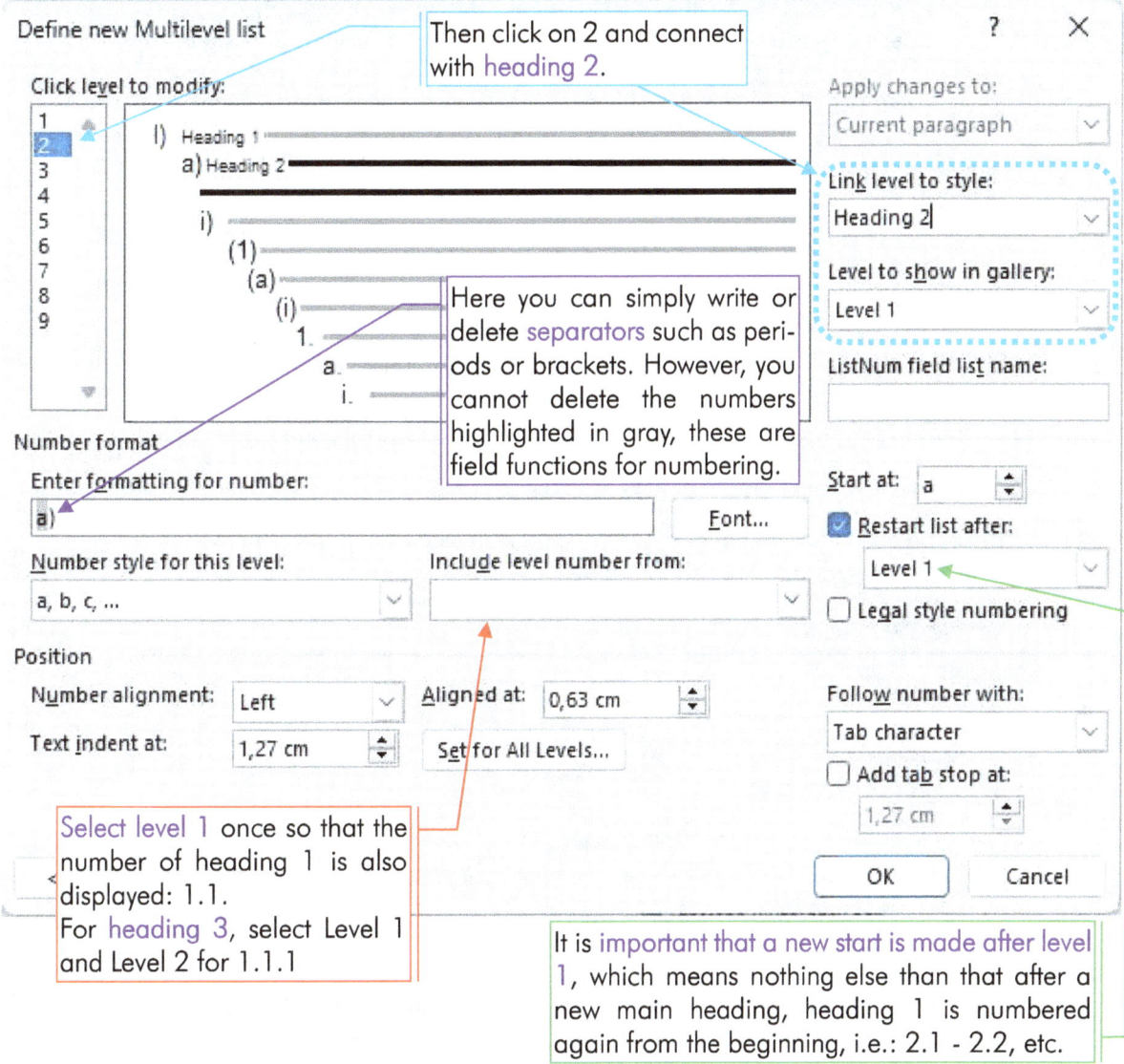

> ➢ Do the same again for the 3rd level = heading 3, here you start again after level 2 and include the level number of headings 1 and 2.

> ✎ Try for example 1.1.a or 1.1.**A**) (the A particularly bold).

Miscellaneous:

♦ Dots, commas, etc. can be written easily, but other numbers can only be selected below them when using a number style... so that they are inserted as a field and Word continues to count in the text.

♦ Setting for all levels...: e.g. the set numbers at -0.2 are transferred into the left margin of all headings right-justified.

♦ Apply changes for: instead of "Complete list", e.g. "Document from here" or "Current paragraph", thus different formatted numbering can be set in a document.

♦ Text afterward: a simple distance or nothing can be specified instead of an adjustable tabulator.

13.5 Adjust Indentations

➢ The easiest way to correct the indentation for a heading with the mouse in the ruler is to use the mouse, if the Update automatically option is selected in the style sheet, this will be taken over into the style sheet.

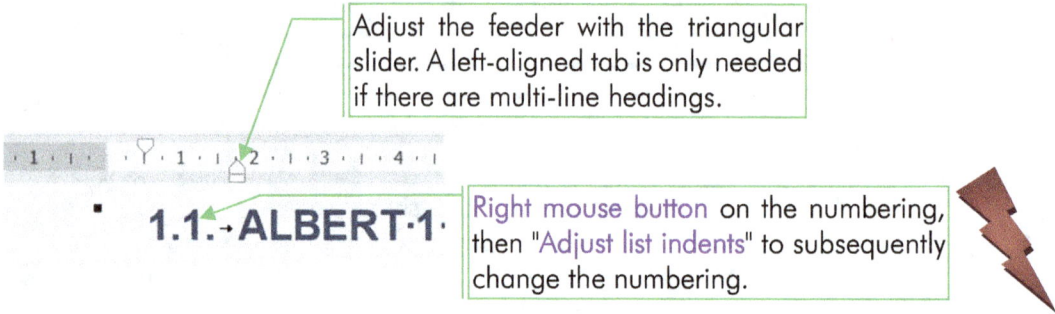

Adjust the feeder with the triangular slider. A left-aligned tab is only needed if there are multi-line headings.

Right mouse button on the numbering, then "Adjust list indents" to subsequently change the numbering.

13.5.1 Set number format/indents in the menu

Interesting formatting of the numbers is, if they are right-aligned in the margin, the text of the heading begins left-aligned.

The first text indent:

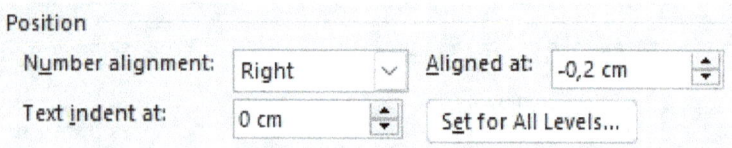

♦ Under Position, the location of the numbers and the text can be adjusted. For example, the headlines are justified as in this book and the numbers are on the left:

   ✍ Right number alignment,

   ✍ Alignment (for the number) -0.2 negative values cannot be selected here with the arrows, but can be entered using the keyboard,

   ✍ Text indent at 0, i.e. so as the text begins at the left margin.

All Headings start with left-justified, the numbers will have the same distance of 2 millimeters, even from 10, because right-justified, i.e. the right margin remains the same and the number will be extended to the left.

13.6 Error in the Table of Contents

If you find an error in the table of contents, never correct it there, but correct the text in the headline. Otherwise, you would have the error in the table of contents again after the next update.

Blank paragraph marks with headings 1, 2 or 3 shall be duly inserted in the table of contents with the chapter number and page number as soon as the headings are numbered at the latest.

Therefore, only use blank paragraphs with the Default or Body Style sheet from the outset.

13.6.1 Update Page Numbers

If you change the text or for instance, the font in order to move the pages, the page numbers will no longer match the table of contents.

- ♦ Word updates the page numbers of the table of contents when a text is opened as well as

- ♦ before every printing unless File/Options/Advanced for Print "Allow fields containing tracked changes to update before printing" is disabled.

13.7 Table of Contents Exercise

The following exercise is about Creating and Customizing a Table of Contents.

Start a new Exercise Text:

- ➤ Write a paragraph, copy it and create about 20 pages of text, then add about twenty headings.

  - ✎ There are four heading levels desired this time.

- ➤ You can assign the heading style sheets using the [Alt]-1, 2, 3 shortcuts,

- ➤ for the fourth heading, you can assign the key combination [Alt]-4 in the Style sheet menu (extension arrow for start style sheets) with right mouse button changes for format/key combination.

- ➤ Here in the style menu you can set visible Heading 4:

- ➤ Set headline style sheets appropriately, especially a distance before the main headlines.

- ➤ Numbering the headings as follows: Heading 1: Chapter A, Heading 2: A-1, Heading 3: A-1.1, Heading 4: A-1.1.a

Create Table of Contents:

- ➤ Add a title page at the beginning and then a second page for the table of contents,

- ➤ Insert the table of contents there, but specify 4 in the Display table of contents menu under Layers.

Format Table of Contents:

The style sheets from directory 1 to 4 are used in the table of contents.

- ➤ Format the main headings in the table of contents with a frame of 60% dark blue and white text, spacing before at least 18 pt using 14 point font size,

- ➤ format the subheadings 2 with small caps and only 11 points font size,

- ➤ set the headings three and four indented respectively.

- ➤ Adjust the table of contents so that it fills the page optimally and print only the table of contents and the title page.

14. Header, Section break

14.1 A Section Break

The opening credits, at least the first two pages, title page and table of contents, should usually remain without a header for each text, which is why we introduce the Section Break. This will be dealt with in more detail in the third volume.

- ♦ For Word, a section break means that differently formatted pages now follow, such as

    ↳ the text continues with a different Header or Footer

    ↳ or the column setting or the page format is to be set differently.

To Practice:

- ➢ Go to the end of the Table of Contents in Chapter 13.

- ➢ Delete the Page Break.

---------------------------------------Page Break---------------------------------------

- ♦ On the Layout tab page, you can set a section break to the next page which is a section break combined with a page break.

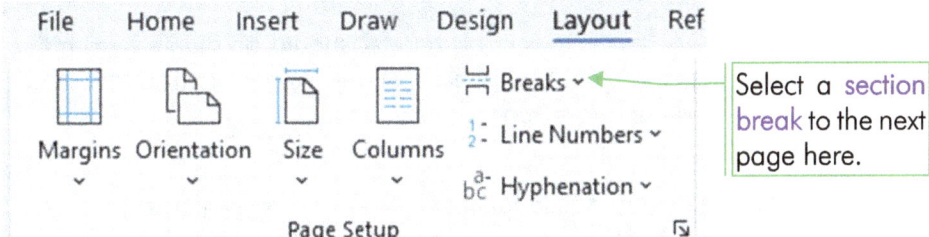

Now we have two sections in the text. We want the header to appear in the second section but not in the first.

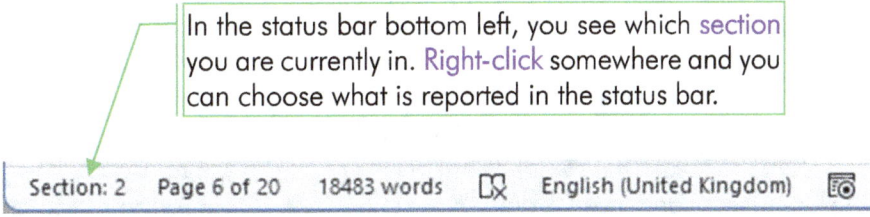

14.2 The Header Line

A header line is automatically repeated on the following pages as well as the footer line at the bottom. A section break is required to change the header or footer.

File   Home   **Insert**   Draw   Design

➢ Go to the page after the table of contents. This is the first page where you want a header to appear.

➢ You will find buttons for the header and footer on the Insert tab.

Header   Footer   Page Number

Header & Footer

✎ Here you can select one of the many default settings or set them up manually with "Edit header".

➢ Choose Edit Header:

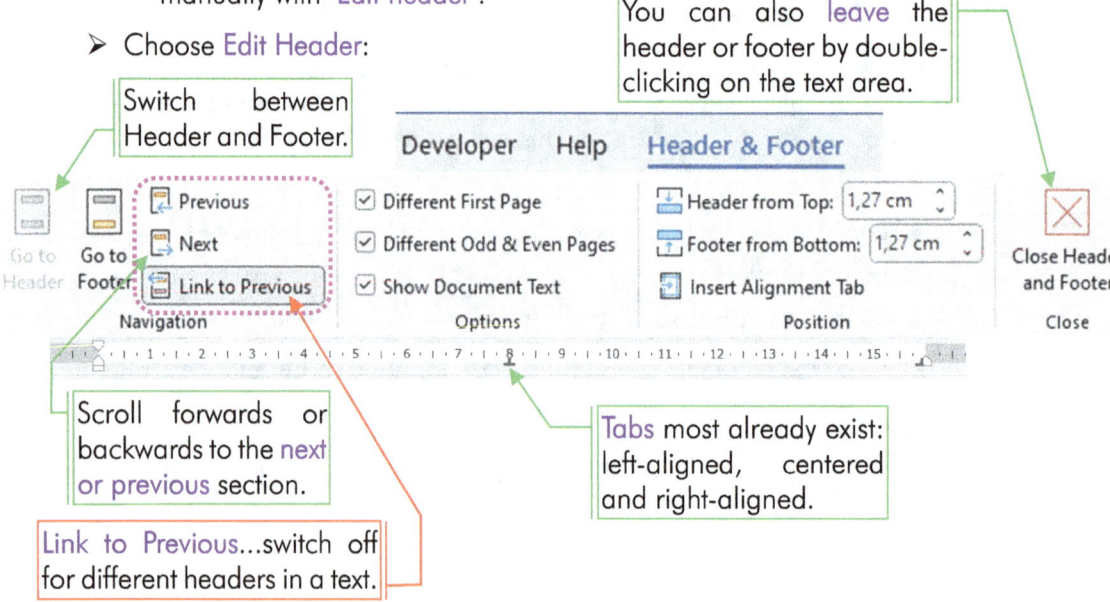

Switch between Header and Footer.

You can also leave the header or footer by double-clicking on the text area.

Scroll forwards or backwards to the next or previous section.

Link to Previous...switch off for different headers in a text.

Tabs most already exist: left-aligned, centered and right-aligned.

!!!!!!!!!!! Important !!!!!!!!!!!

Switch off "Link to previous"! This header should be different from the empty headers of the first pages. This setting option is the most common cause of errors in header lines.

➢ In order to become a little familiar with the many switches, you should create the following header, but page 4 with the main chapter without, page 5 with the first header:

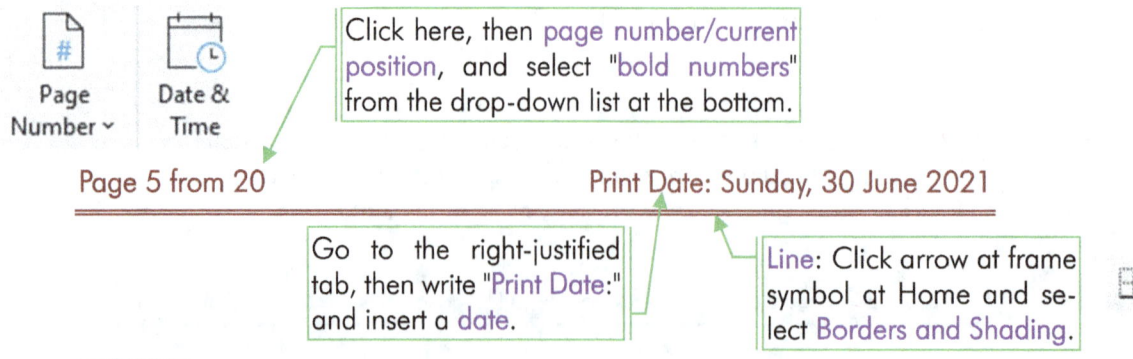

Click here, then page number/current position, and select "bold numbers" from the drop-down list at the bottom.

Page 5 from 20   Print Date: Sunday, 30 June 2021

Go to the right-justified tab, then write "Print Date:" and insert a date.

Line: Click arrow at frame symbol at Home and select Borders and Shading.

14.2.1 Header Functions Exercise

➢ Delete everything and place the following in the header this time:

Your Name   Page 5   30.06.19

➢ To do this, use all three existing tabs or simply reset them as described in the first volume.

↳ Then overwrite the data using the page number as function and the date with Insert/Date and Time.

➢ Delete the page number in the header and place it on the right side of the footer in an attractive format.

14.2.2 Setting up the Header and Footer

You will find these setting options in the header menu:

Help	Header & Footer
☑ Different First Page	
☑ Different Odd & Even Pages	
☑ Show Document Text	
	Options

It means:

♦ Different First-Page means that you can enter a different header line (or none at all) on this first page (each section).

↳ This is the standard that no header is printed at the beginning of a main chapter (=empty header with Different First Page).

↳ The header from the second page is repeated in the rest of the document. This option is still available for this:

♦ Different Odd & Even Pages are to check if you want to set up the headers and footers differently on both sides, which is usually the case when the paper is printed on both sides.

↳ This is usually necessary because the page numbers should be on the outside, i.e. on a left side on the outside left and on the right side on the outside right.

↳ Of course, you can save yourself this option and the associated adjustment work by setting the page numbers at the center.

Even and odd pages:

♦ Open a book:

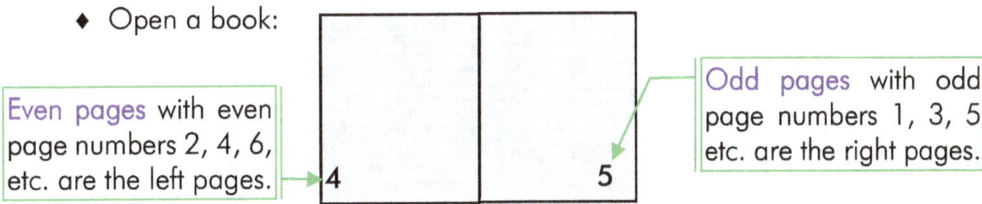

Even pages with even page numbers 2, 4, 6, etc. are the left pages. → 4   5   Odd pages with odd page numbers 1, 3, 5 etc. are the right pages.

♦ A new chapter should always start on a right and odd page, if necessary leave the previous left page blank.

Different headers for books and brochures are presented in the third volume.

14.2.3 The Header Position

If the header line is larger, e.g. because it contains a lot of text and the space for the normal text is automatically reduced because it always starts below the header line. For the header line, therefore, only the distance from the paper edge is specified, not the size.

- If the header is open, the starting position of the header or footer can be specified in the "Header & Footer" tab at the top:

  - How much space the header or footer actually occupies depends on the content entered.

    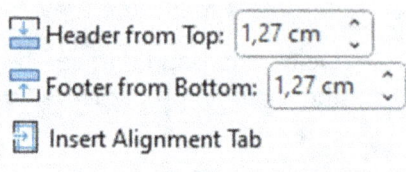

  - Correspondingly, there is less space available for the text if there is a lot of text or large font.

  - If the header line is to be intentionally enlarged, insert empty paragraph marks or a paragraph spacing if necessary.

Opposite pages:

- You can also set the header and footer size as well as the paper layout on the Layout tab of the Size/More Paper Sizes.

  - If you want to print on both sides of the paper, you must select "Mirror Margins" under "Multiple pages:" on the tab Margins, and under "Apply to" you can select the area for which this setting is to apply: This section, this point forward or a whole document.

Overview of header and footer spacing:

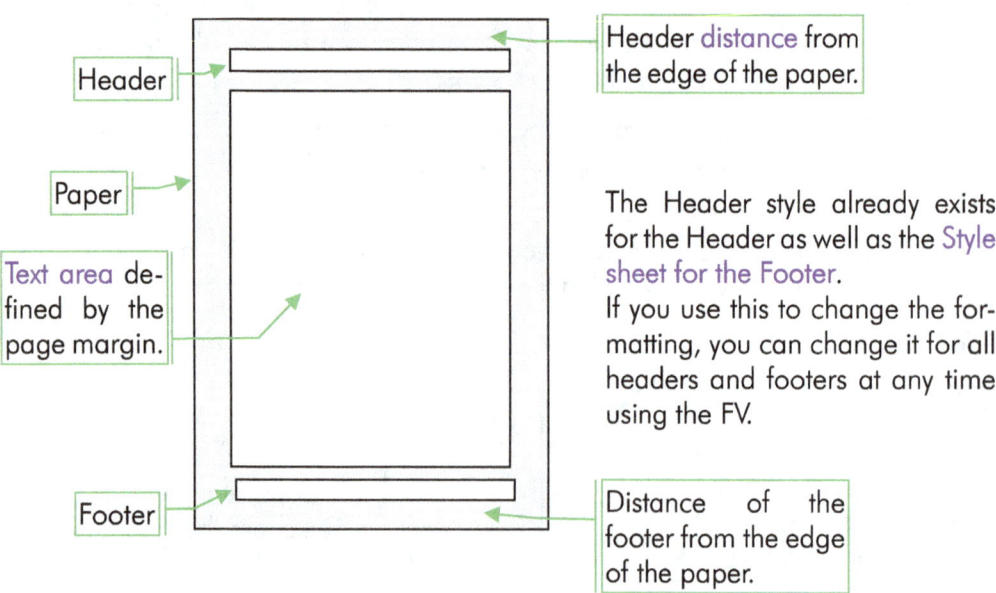

The Header style already exists for the Header as well as the Style sheet for the Footer.
If you use this to change the formatting, you can change it for all headers and footers at any time using the FV.

If text is truncated below:

- Most printers cannot print approx. 1.3 cm at the bottom edge. Refer to the printer manual for the non-printable area.

15. Footnotes

Footnotes are at the end of the page while Endnotes are at the end of the Text which otherwise performs the same function for annotations, source references, or other additional information.

15.1 Insert Footnotes

We stick to the "Table of Contents" exercise of the previous chapter.

➤ Place the cursor immediately after Einstein (in the first paragraph).

✎ Of course, if there is still a header open, close it first by double-clicking on the text or symbol.

➤ Select References on the tab: Insert footnote.

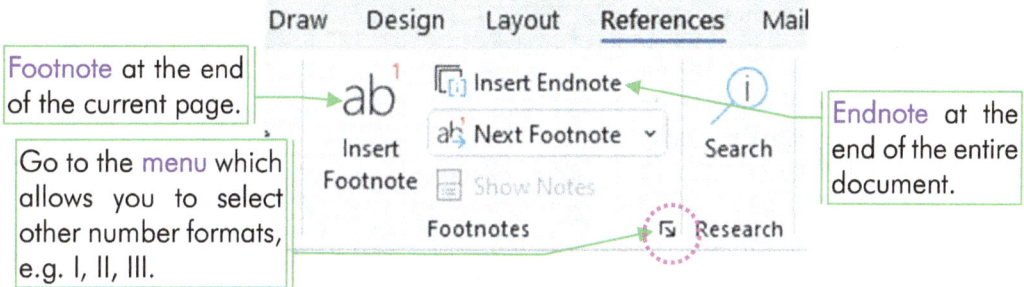

➤ Search for the red marked words and add some footnote texts.

If you can't think of anything and these notes are not too long, here are some text suggestions for the footnotes:

1. *Albert Einstein:* Developed the theory of relativity.
2. *Charles Darwin:* Founder of the theory of evolution.
3. *Leibniz:* Universal scholar, 1646-1716, developed the dual number system that every computer uses today.
4. *Nietzsche:* 1844-1900, German philosopher, also defined morality as a means of power and enforcement.
5. "*Those who would give up essential Liberty, to purchase a little temporary Safety, deserve neither Liberty nor Safety.*": Benjamin Franklin
6. *Michel Foucault:* the consensus in a community as the truth of this community.

> Double-click on the footnote number to navigate between text and footnotes.

The menu can be opened with the small extension arrow, for instance, to set the number format of the Footnotes and Endnotes:

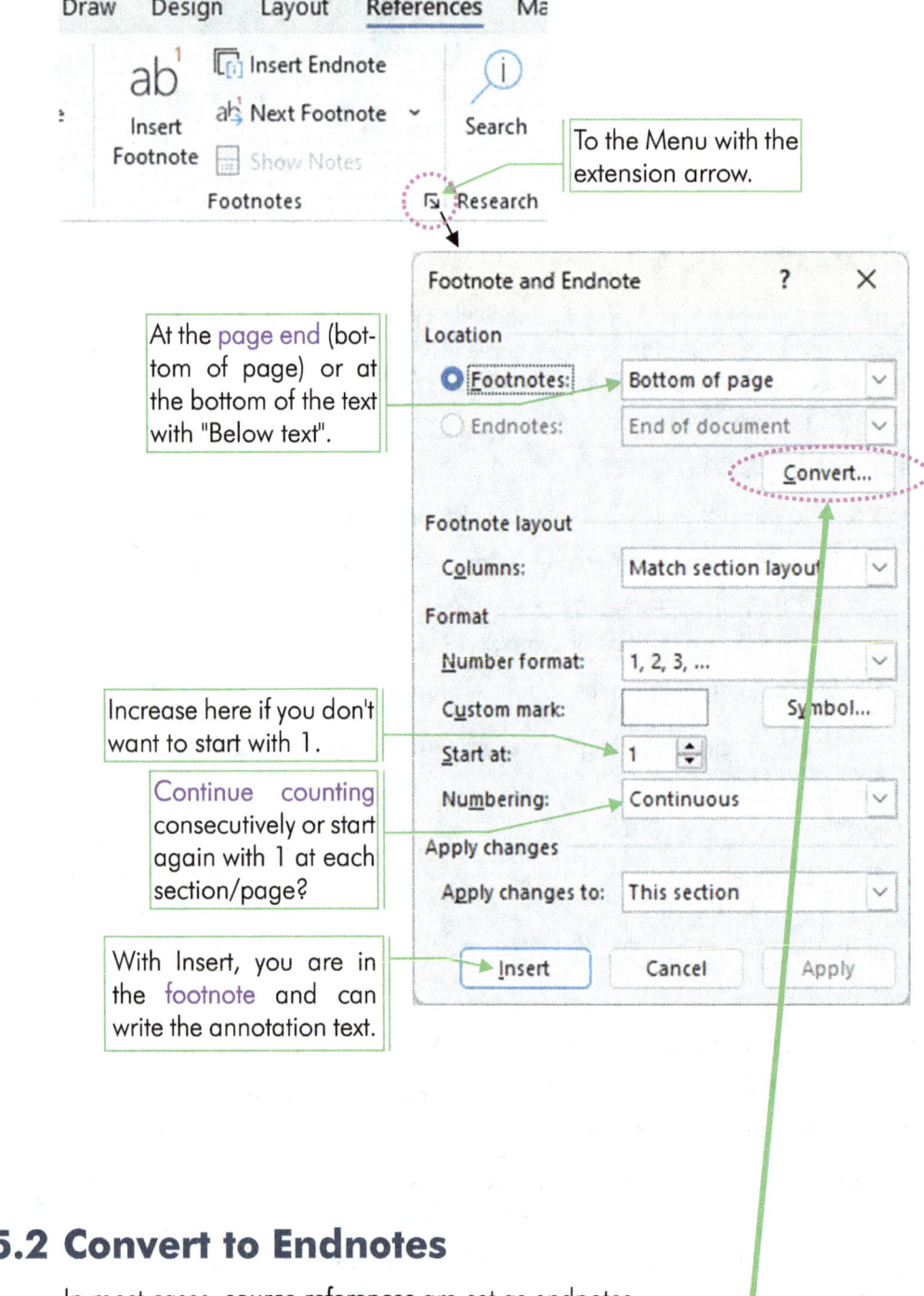

At the page end (bottom of page) or at the bottom of the text with "Below text".

To the Menu with the extension arrow.

Increase here if you don't want to start with 1.

Continue counting consecutively or start again with 1 at each section/page?

With Insert, you are in the footnote and can write the annotation text.

15.2 Convert to Endnotes

In most cases, **source references** are set as endnotes.

♦ Now you have footnotes under each page. Very convenient is the ability to **convert** footnotes to endnotes and vice versa.

  ✍ This allows you, for example, to enter source information directly on the page and gives you a good overview,

  ✍ and convert them at the bottom into Endnote, which is summarized at the end of the text.

Convert a single Footnote:

- ♦ Press the right mouse button on the Footnote text and select "Convert to Endnotes".

Convert all Footnotes:

- ➢ Reopen the menu and select the Convert button.

  - ↳ For extensive texts (books, brochures, etc.), each chapter is usually a separate section to enable different entries in the header. If you activate Endnotes at the end of the section, they will appear at the end of the chapter.

- ➢ Convert all footnotes to endnotes and check the result.

  - ↳ Obviously, you can also undo such actions or convert endnotes back to footnotes.

15.3 Formatting Endnotes or Footnotes

Footnotes also have their own style sheet called footnote text, and endnotes have their own endnote text. You should, therefore, use this style sheet to set the footnotes.

The following style sheets are available for footnotes and endnotes:

- ♦ Footnote text: Footnotes are at the bottom of the page.

  - ↳ Footnote reference mark: Style sheet for the footnote numbers.

- ♦ Endnote text: End notes are at the end of the text or section. Section breaks will be described in detail in volume 3.

  - ↳ Endnotes characters: Style sheet for the numbers of the endnotes.

However, these style sheets are not initially displayed.

- ➢ Therefore, press the right mouse button on the footnote or endnote text and select the Style sheet.

- ➢ In the menu that appears, select Change.

- ➢ Change the style sheet Endnote text as follows: Font size 8pt with distance before/after of 2 pt.

- ➢ Set the hanging indent in the Endnote text style sheet on the Paragraph tab.

> The hanging indent cannot be set up via the numbering because the numbers would then be there twice. Therefore, the indentation must be set manually in the style sheet.

An additional tabulator must be set so that the text is aligned exactly with each other in the case of several lines.

➢ To do this, press Tab in the paragraph menu. The following applies: hanging by 0.3 cm, therefore tabulator also at 0.3 cm.

➢ Set a tab after each endnote number.

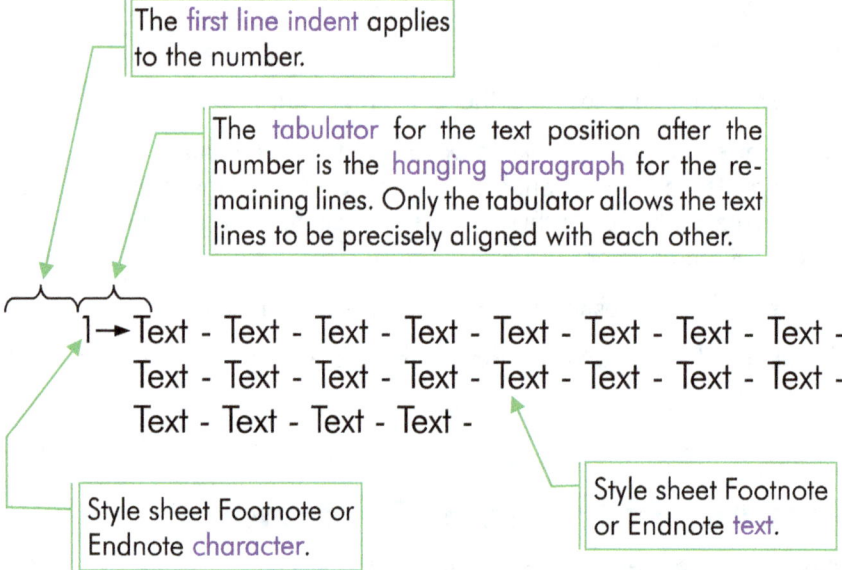

The first line indent applies to the number.

The tabulator for the text position after the number is the hanging paragraph for the remaining lines. Only the tabulator allows the text lines to be precisely aligned with each other.

Style sheet Footnote or Endnote character.

Style sheet Footnote or Endnote text.

➢ The footnote or endnote character style sheet is only displayed after you have set it with the right mouse button/Style. For example, change the color of the numbers.

15.4 Number Lines

Before we close our long text exercise, we can try the line numbering which can be activated on the Layout tab:

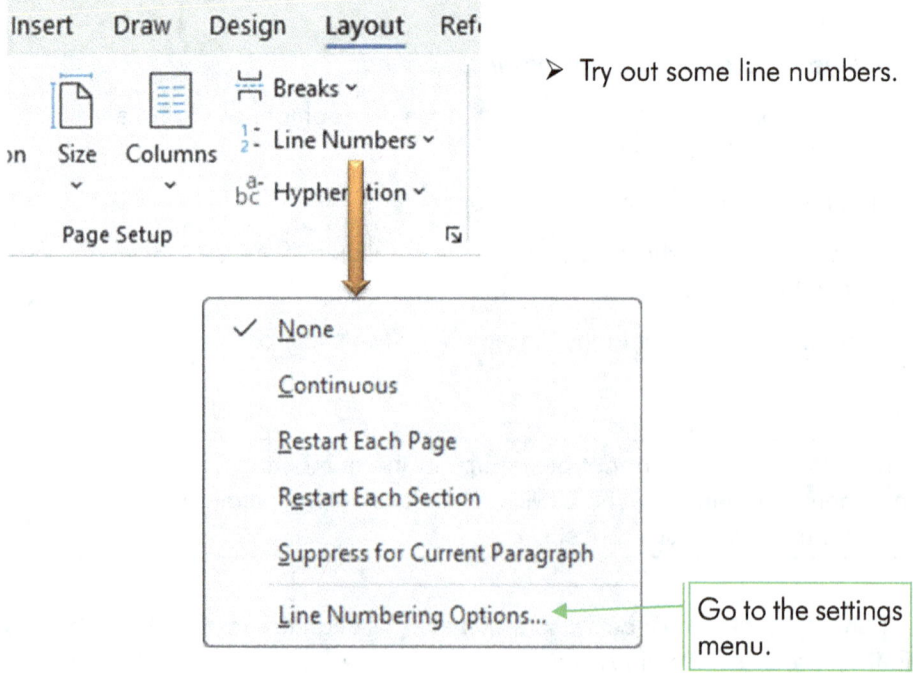

➢ Try out some line numbers.

Go to the settings menu.

Part Five

Serial Printing

rational Working: Serial Letters, Envelopes and Labels Printing

16. Serial Letters

Afraid of serial letters? Not anymore longer. We can open an existing document which should then become our serial letter or start the mail merge function and create a new letter or select an existing letter from the mail merge menu.

16.1 As an Illustration

With serial printing, you do not manually put an address in a letter for printing. Instead, you have a letter in which addresses are automatically inserted from a database.

It doesn't matter whether it is a letter, an email or an envelope, or whether you want to create a new database or use an existing one.

The Database:

Name	First name	Street
Sample	Walter	Avenue 31
Muller	Jon	Seastr. 44

One address (=one data record) is set in a letter and printed. The letter contains fields (»first name« etc.) as placeholders.

The **Letter** (main document)

»first name« »last name«
«street»

«postcode» «city»

Text ... Text ...

Therefore, these three steps must be carried out one after the other:

♦ The actual serial letter (or envelope etc.),

♦ then the data source with the addresses must be created or opened,

  ↳ Fields in the main document specify where each data from the data source is to be inserted,

♦ and finally, the actual action can be started as often as you like, in which an address is placed in a letter and printed.

16.2 A business letter

We will first create a practice letter to make it clearer. Since serial letters are almost always of a business nature and are produced in large quantities, it is a good idea to design a letter in accordance with the standards. Actual standards you find e.g. in Wikipedia, search for business letter.

16.2.1 Page Setup (Layout/Page Setup)

- In a new document, all margins should be between 1 and 1 1/4 inch.
  - ✍ You can enter the Letterhead in the header line to protect it from unintentional changes.
  - ✍ Then you would enter 2 inch as the top margin for the sender and ¾ inch for the header on the Layout tab, but it depends how many lines and how big you want your letterhead.
  - ✍ The U.S. paper size is 8.5 x 11 inch = 216 x 279 cm.
- ➢ Enter a letterhead in the header line:

  - ✍ This sender address can be freely designed and also embellished with WordArt.
  - ✍ Add a logo, e.g. via WordArt.

> My Example Ltd.
> Workstreet 1
> 01234 Big City
> www.myexample.com
> email@myexymple.com

16.2.2 The Address

The address with the sender's details should fit well into the viewing window, although in the case of business mail merge documents, it should be noted that as a rule, there are many addresses with additional lines, such as the company address or department. Therefore, it is better to start at the top of the envelope window and do not select a too large font.

- The position of the address block: Measure the viewing window from your usual envelope, then apply this measure for the address block in the mailing list.
- Use a small font and a dividing line to indicate the sender address above the address area, so that the letter can return if necessary.

The correct Address:[4]

To one person:	To a Company:
1. Annotations, e.g. Personal	1. Annotations and Additions, e.g. Personal
2. Annotations, e.g. Personal	2. Annotations and Additions, e.g. Personal
3. e.g. Registered mail	3. Form of dispatch, e.g. by registered mail
4.	4. Company
5.Salutation, Title	5. Salutation
6.First name Surname	6. Contact person
7. Street	7. Street, P.O. Box
8. Postcode and City	8. Postcode and City
9. Country	9. Country

---

[4] Address formats by country and area: https://en.wikipedia.org/wiki/Address

16.2.3 A Specimen Letter

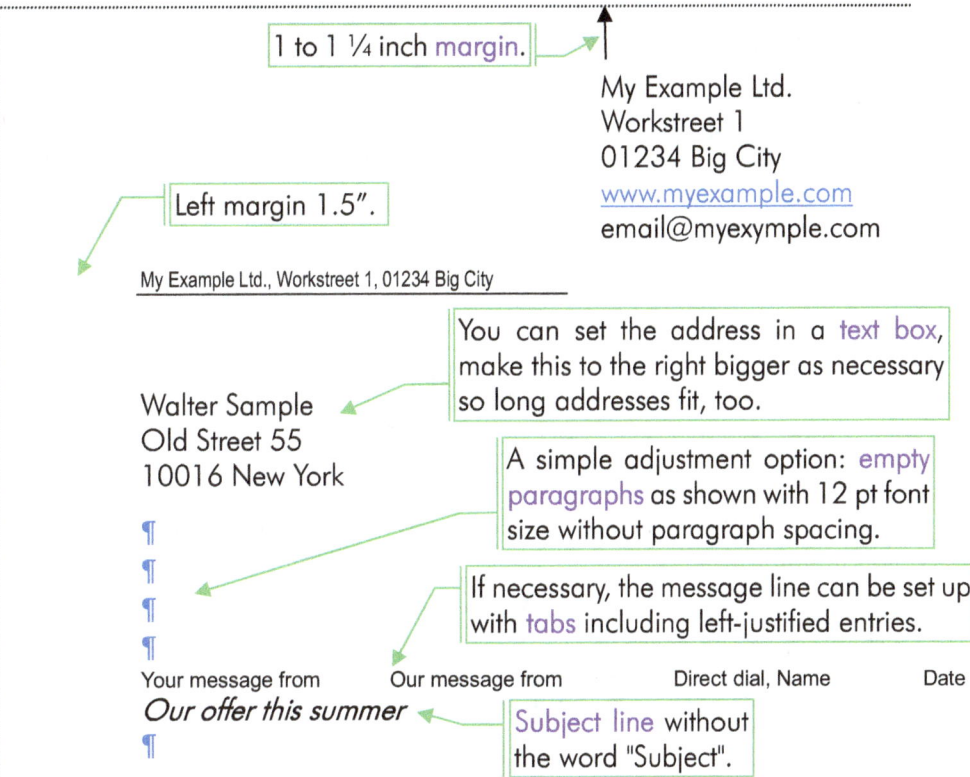

> ➢ The message line is followed by the subject line, but the word subject is currently no longer written.

> ➢ Before the text of the letter, write the salutation "Dear Ladies, Dear Gentlemen," and at the end "With kind regards".

>> ✍ Obviously, better than this impersonal address is: "Dear Mr. Anton Receiver". Such differentiated salutations followed in the third volume in the query conditions for serial letters.

Dear Madam,
Dear Sir,

¶

This is where the letter text begins...

> ➢ At the bottom of the page, preferably in the footer, enter some more details including the bank details in the footer of a business letter.

>> ✍ With a centered and a right-aligned tab, everything can be arranged as shown.

Phone:111 12345678-12	My bank	Management: Anton Example
Telefax:111 12345678-9	Account-No. 11111	AG New York HRB 11111
email@myexample.com	SORT CODE 111 111 11	VAT ID No. DE0000 111 111
www.myexample.com	IBAN: 1234 1234 1234 1234 1234 12	Tax No. 345/234XX

> ➢ Simply save this letter to a folder called "Letters", then open this letter later and with Save file as open, customize and save under a suitable file name. This is more convenient than creating a document template.

16.3 Create the Data Source

Let's start converting the letter into a serial print document.

➢ First delete the sample adress and set the cursor at this place.

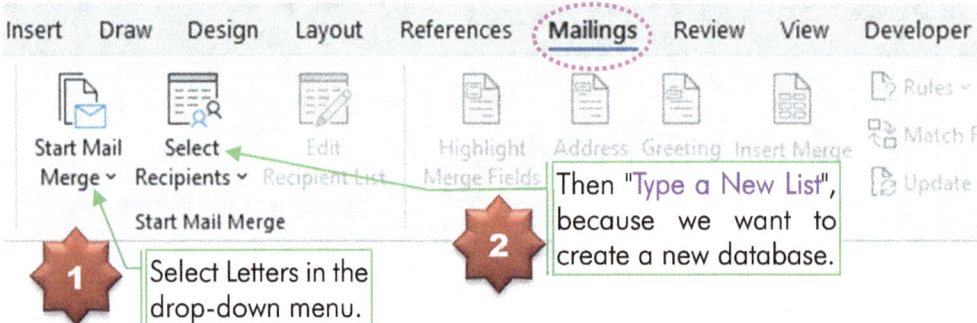

- In the drop-down list, you can see that emails, envelopes, labels, etc. can also be created as serial documents, e.g. to print addresses directly onto envelopes.

- You can select also an existing database as the data source instead of creating a new data list.

An input window for the first data is displayed:

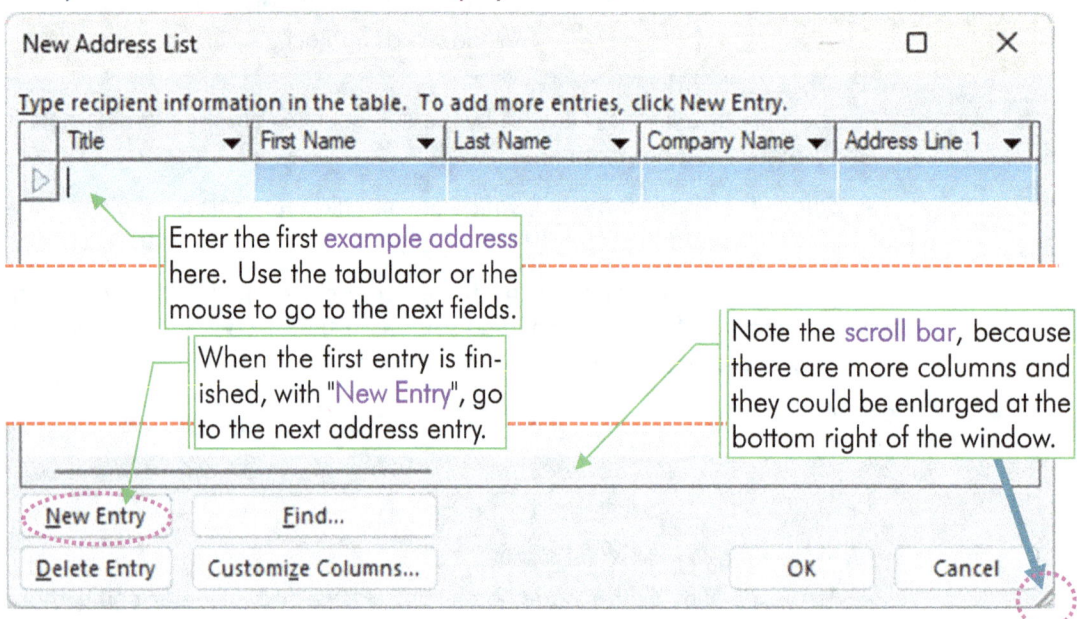

For example, enter these three sample addresses:

Title	First Name	Last Name	Address line 1	ZIP	City	Work Phone
Mr.	Walter	Sample	250 Utica Ave	11213	New York	+17182524666
Ms.	Antonia	Muller	15009 Flanders St	48205	Detroit	
Mr.	Sam	Smith	15301 McNab Ave	90706	Los Angeles	

Let's use the given fields to avoid too much at the beginning. We will explain later on page 99 how to rename, delete or add new fields.

16.3.1 Save database

If you press "Close", the database is automatically saved.

> ➢ The save window appears, save the database in our exercise folder letters with the filename "SampleAddressList".

16.4 Edit Data Source

We should now practice how to reopen the database to include more records or correct errors.

Edit Recipient List

◆ Although the database is saved in MS Access format mdb, it can still be further processed in MS Word.

➢ Select "Edit Recipient List",

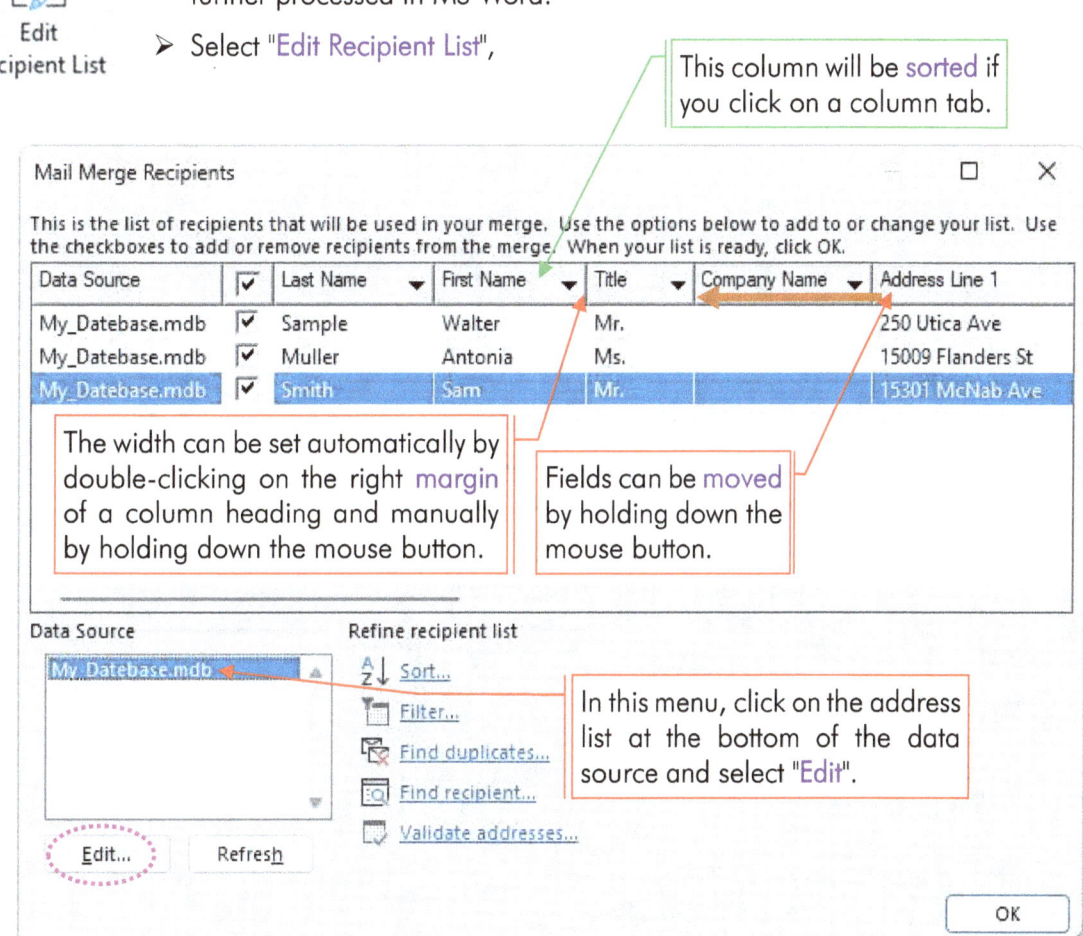

This column will be sorted if you click on a column tab.

The width can be set automatically by double-clicking on the right margin of a column heading and manually by holding down the mouse button.

Fields can be moved by holding down the mouse button.

In this menu, click on the address list at the bottom of the data source and select "Edit".

> ➢ Enter additional addresses for the exercise:

Each line is a Data Set.

The column heading is the field name.

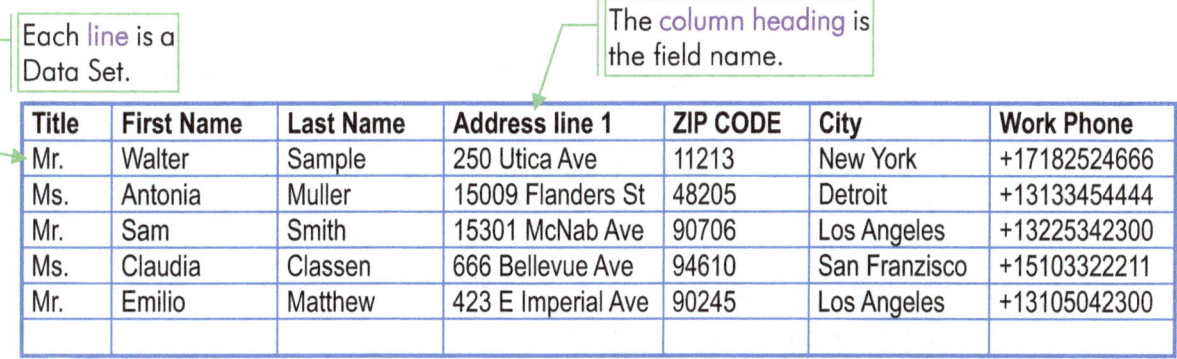

Title	First Name	Last Name	Address line 1	ZIP CODE	City	Work Phone
Mr.	Walter	Sample	250 Utica Ave	11213	New York	+17182524666
Ms.	Antonia	Muller	15009 Flanders St	48205	Detroit	+13133454444
Mr.	Sam	Smith	15301 McNab Ave	90706	Los Angeles	+13225342300
Ms.	Claudia	Classen	666 Bellevue Ave	94610	San Franzisco	+15103322211
Mr.	Emilio	Matthew	423 E Imperial Ave	90245	Los Angeles	+13105042300

16.4.1 Edit new Fields and Fields

In the previous menu, you can not only add new fields but also rename, delete or optimize the sequence of existing fields under "Customize columns":

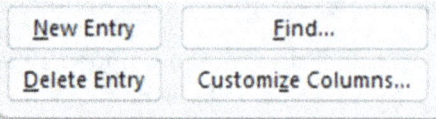

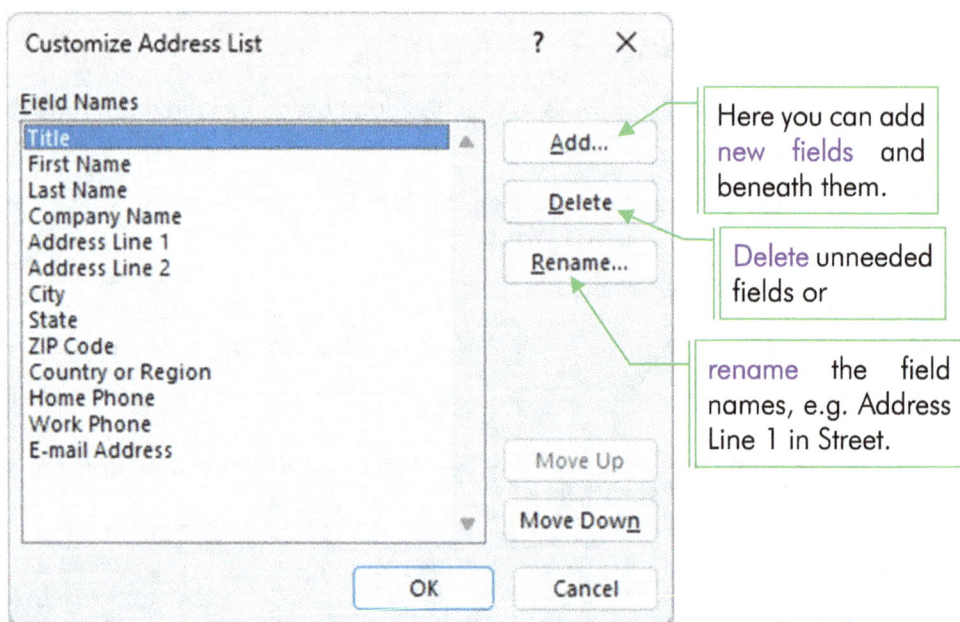

➢ After the salutation, add a new Title field and rename address line 1 to Street, address line 2 to No (a dot does not work as a field name) and correct the entries.

➢ Change the order of the fields meaningfully, e.g., "Last Name" first, then "Title", "First Name", etc.

1.1 Thesaurus

The Thesaurus helps you to find words with similar meanings.

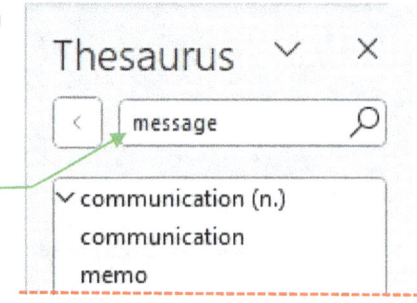

Enter a word here and alternatives will be searched as soon as you press Return or click on the magnifying glass.

You can start the Thesaurus in three ways:

♦ Via the menu under Review/Thesaurus.

♦ Or right-click on the word and select "Synonyms/Thesaurus" from the drop-down list.

♦ The last variant is the keyboard shortcut [Shift]-F7. This is not that hard to remember, because F7 is the spellchecker.

Also, note the possibility to search for synonyms in other languages at the bottom of the Thesaurus.

17. Complete Mail Merge

Then you can return to the mail merge and set up the mail merge. Word can be used to do this, e.g. by inserting the address block or the salutation completely formatted.

➢ First, place the cursor on the desired position, then you can

✍ prefabricated address block

✍ or select a greeting line (Dear ...)

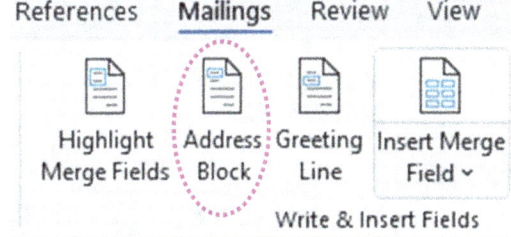

✍ or arrange the fields for the address itself appropriately (insert Merge Field).

The Address Block:

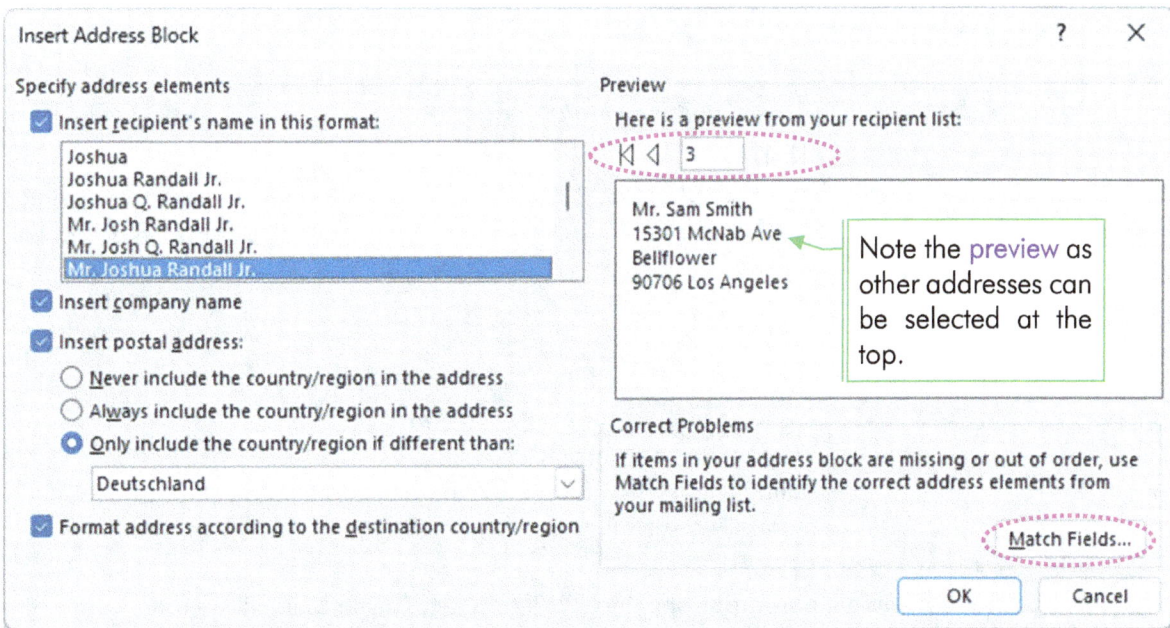

No matter which defaults setting you chose on the left, the finished address blocks are not always optimal, so we are going to practice creating the address ourselves.

➢ Select the Address Block/Match Fields option.

➢ As shown on the next page, you must select the correct fields on the right for the address to be displayed correctly.

The fields must be filled-in appropriately:

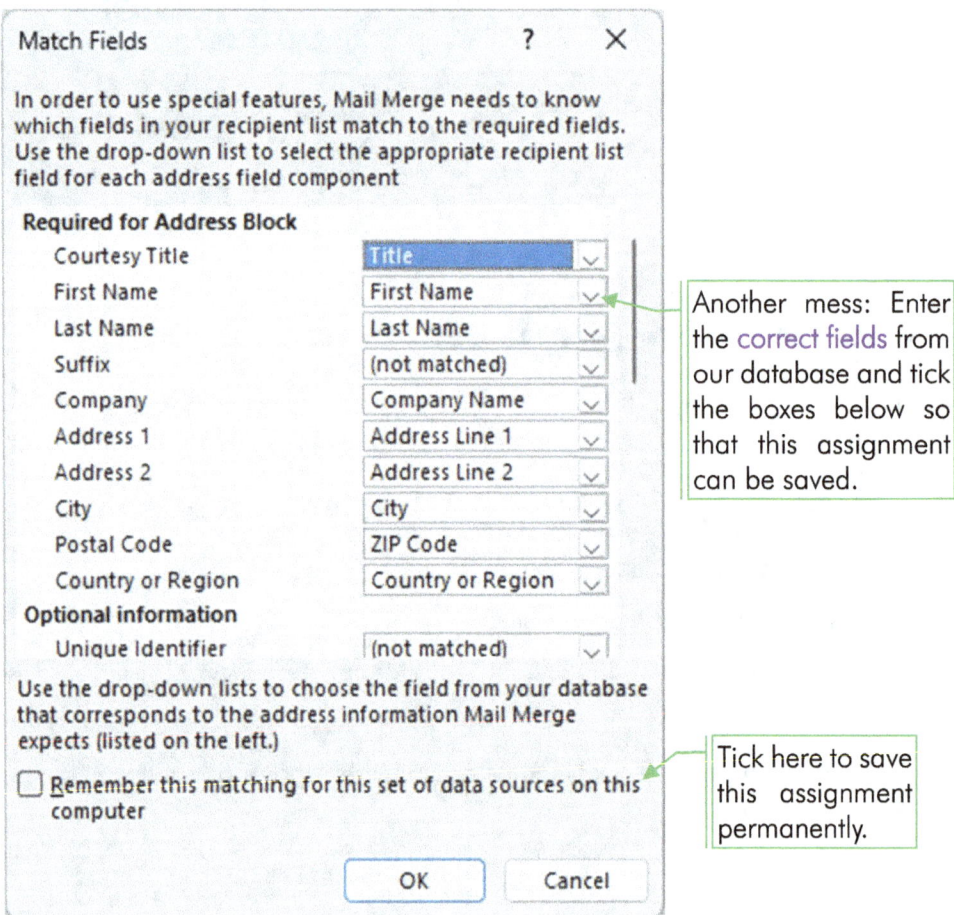

Another mess: Enter the correct fields from our database and tick the boxes below so that this assignment can be saved.

Tick here to save this assignment permanently.

This will be done in the serial document after OK:

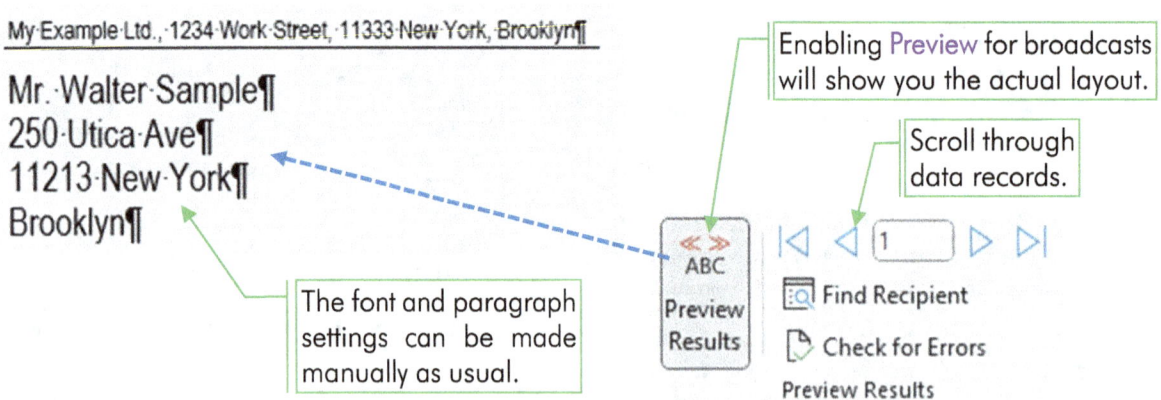

Enabling Preview for broadcasts will show you the actual layout.

Scroll through data records.

The font and paragraph settings can be made manually as usual.

➢ Set up: without paragraph spacing, Postcode and City in bold with 14pt font size.

The completed address block and greeting line, therefore, require some adjustments until everything fits as desired so that it is usually easier to manually compile the address.

➢ Obviously, for comparison and practice, you can insert the address block and then manually arrange the fields below it again using the following procedure.

17.1 Set up Address and Fields

The address block does not necessarily save work, it is often easier to manually compile an address. In this way, all existing data in the serial document can be used anywhere in the document, e.g. to find out whether a telephone number is still correct.

Delete address blocks and compile an address manually:

➢ Close the mail merge window with the X symbol, delete the inserted address, then move the cursor to the address position in the letter.

➢ Press the "Insert Merge Field" icon (or "More Items" from the wizard), then select the first "Salutation" field.

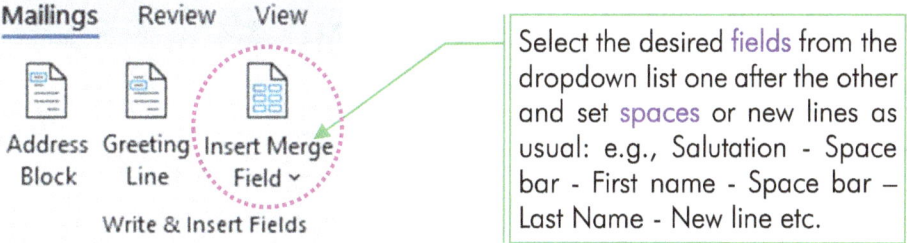

Select the desired fields from the dropdown list one after the other and set spaces or new lines as usual: e.g., Salutation - Space bar - First name - Space bar – Last Name - New line etc.

My·Example·Ltd.,·1234·Work·Street,·11333·New·York,·Brooklyn¶

Ms.··Antonia·Muller¶
15009·Flanders·St¶
48205·Detroit¶

So, it is best to set the fields immediately when the preview is activated, then you will see the result instead of the fields.

Without Preview you see the fields:

My·Example·Ltd.,·1234·Work·Street,·11333·New·York,·Brooklyn¶

«Title»·«First_Name»·«Last_Name»↵
«Street»↵
«ZIP_Code»·«City»↵
«Country_or_Region»¶

We will start the exercise with such a simple address. Several lines will follow later.

17.1.1 Worth knowing about Fields

♦ Fields, e.g. «Surname»: You only have to set the fields as if they were a correct address.

♦ You can treat fields like normal text, i.e. select, format or even cut them and paste them elsewhere.

  ↳ The only important thing is that you always take the «»-field characters with you.

♦ If you select a field, such as »Postal code«, and set a larger font, this applies to all postal codes of mail merge.

Fields are placeholders: the last name from the database is inserted in the Last Name field, the street in the Street field, and so on. A related address is a data set.

17.2 Start Mail Merge

Finally, all that remains is to execute the mail merge. An address is inserted into a letter and printed, automatically followed by the next address, and so on. (=connecting the addresses with the letter).

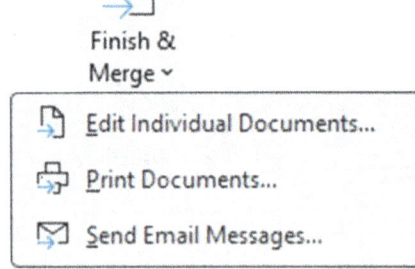

> ➤ Always check with the preview function first.
> At least some addresses should be checked.

> ➤ Then start the mail merge by "Finish & Merge", preferably with "edit individual documents" into a new, normal Word document, which you can then view for checking before printing.

>> ✎ This is also a practical method to print only certain addresses. Search for these pages and enter the page numbers in the print menu.

>> ✎ You can also save this new mail merge document so that you can print individual letters from it again later.

♦ Edit Individual Documents…:

>> ✎ It does not print but creates a new text that you can look at for review.

>> ✎ Do not correct here, but always in the original letter, then restart the mail merge.

>> ✎ As a rule, this document should not be saved, since you can recreate it at any time.

> Good for checking, because errors are always noticeable.

♦ Print documents: every serial letter will be printed immediately.

>> ✎ Usually, you notice some impossible errors after thirty pages and start over, so it takes longer than if you first printed into a document for checking.

♦ With the last option, send e-mail messages…,

>> ✎ serial e-mails would be generated instead of serial letters,

>> ✎ the data source must, of course, contain email addresses and "Close" must be selected in the following window.

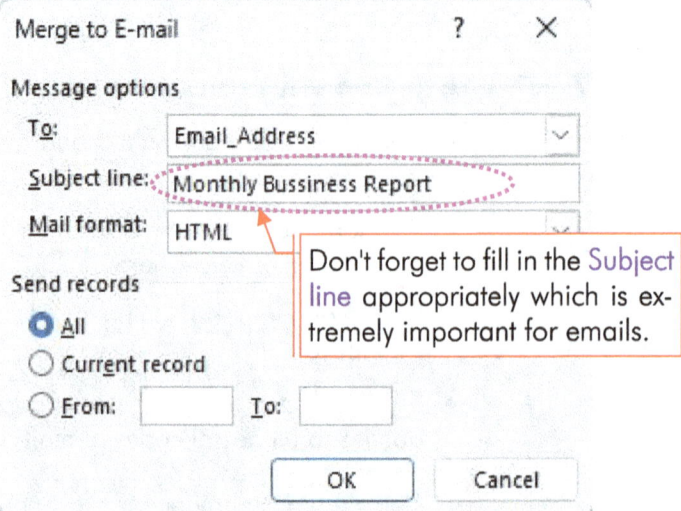

17.3 Tips for large Mail Merge-Actions

To be Corrected:

- Not only view the preview on screen, but also print at least one data set.

  - ✎ Correct this printout thoroughly, because the frustration and loss of time are enormous when hundreds of serial letters have been printed that have to be sent to the waste paper because of small errors!

> Always correct with a sharp printout on paper with time. The display on the screen is significantly worse so that errors that are immediately noticeable on the paper printout are overlooked!

- The person who created the letter must never be the only one who proofreads it.

  - ✎ At least one, preferably two other persons should proofread without time pressure.

  - ✎ Own mistakes are mostly overlooked, no matter how often the text is read!

To Print:

- Printing can take a long time, especially if you have used images or lines.

  - ✎ When the computer prints for twenty minutes, then crashes, the tedious search begins to identify which address was last printed.

- This is a bit easier if you print in stages and sorted into a new document (e.g. postal code from 80000 to 85000).

How does it work?

- The simplest method is to print a new document, save it and then enter the desired page numbers when printing.

  - ✎ In this document, letters that have already been printed can be deleted if necessary.

- Another way is via the filters, which are explained in the third volume on MS Word and in this Special Edition on Serial Letters and Labels.

Simulate an emergency:

When sending as email, the format is converted into HTML format, i.e. something can definitely shift or change. Almost nothing is a bigger disaster than emailing incorrect messages to customers or business partners, especially if it were several hundred or thousands.

> If you start offline (disconnect the WLAN connection, switch off the router or disconnect the network cable), you can have the serial emails created in real life, but since nothing can be sent, you can check them again at your leisure.

17.4 Database as MS Word Table

If you would rather have a database than a normal table in an MS Word document, as was the case with previous Word versions, this is also possible with the following trick.

➢ Select "New document". Create a table in this new document.

    ✎ In this table, the column headings are entered in the first line. The field names are entered later.

    ✎ Important: this table may only exist, no paragraphs in front of the table!

Accept an existing MS Word data table:

If the data table has already been created, you can also select it in the mail merge wizard or for an existing mail merge document using the button shown.

Select
Recipients ⌄

Edit a Word Data Table:

If you use a Word document with a table as the data source, it is easier to edit or print it in Word.

◆ Simply open this document to edit a Word data table. In this table, you can work like in any other table:

    ✎ Add new Lines (=Datasets),

    ✎ Delete Lines, Change Data, etc.

    ✎ You can even use all table tools to make the table more beautiful and possibly printable.

◆ You can also insert a new field in the database language by entering the name of the new field in the first line of the column.

◆ You can also change field names (= column headers).

    ✎ Delete the old field name and insert it again if the field is already used in a document.

◆ Landscape format is suitable for printing which can be selected for page layout orientation.

Note: ....
....
....
....
....
....
....
....
....
....
....
....
....

18. Create Labels

♦ We merged a data set with a letter in the mail merge.

    ↳ The data sets for labels are only put together differently and exactly match the label stickers.

♦ Usually, you only need to specify the type of label you are using because all standard label formats are already saved in Word.

    ↳ The cumbersome work of adapting the printout to the labels is so most time not necessary.

18.1 Using the Mail Merge Wizard

We want to put an address from our database on a label and therefore start this time with the serial print wizard.

Start Mail Merge ˅

➢ Start a new, blank Document.

➢ Use the "Step by Step Mail merge wizard..." tab with Start mail merge tab.

Choose Labels this time.

➢ After Next, you can select the label form under "Label options":

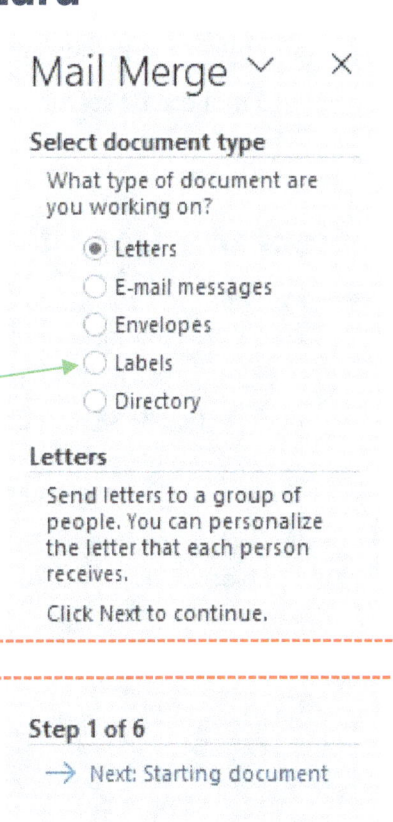

18.2 Select Label Format

You can select the label formats from almost all label manufacturers in the following menu under Label Options. This means the label form is already perfectly set up.

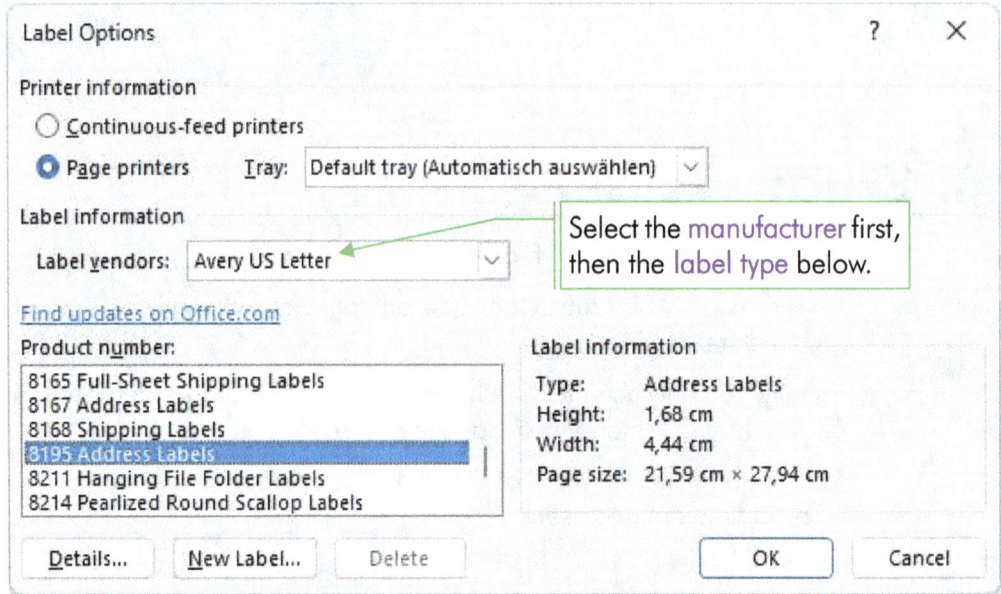

- ◆ The label dimensions can be displayed for checking under Details. You can also change the dimensions in this menu.

- ◆ A format can be set manually for "New label". This involves a lot of work!

18.3 Select the Data Source

➢ We want to use the data source we created in the last exercise, so after "Next... " "Use an existing list."

➢ and with Browse, the database created during the previous mail merge exercise and confirm all data.

   🖑 You can use the checkmarks to select specific addresses in case not all of them are desired.

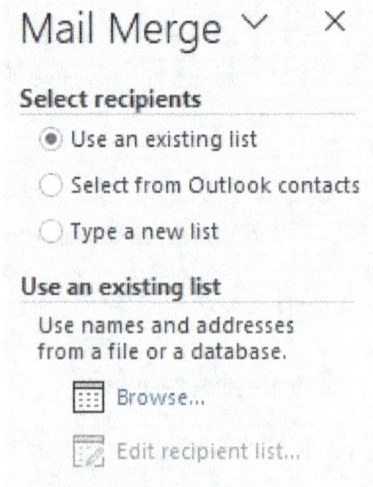

➢ After "Next..." the addresses can be placed on the labels.

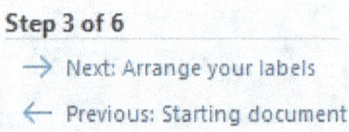

Set up the Document:

> ➢ Add the address block to the first label, check the order of the fields in the preview and correct, if necessary, by "Match Fields").

Mail Merge ∨   ✕

Arrange your labels

If you have not already done so, lay out your label using the first label on the sheet.

To add recipient information to your label, click a location in the first label, and then click one of the items below.

📄 Address block...

📄 Greeting line...

◎ Electronic postage...

🏢 More items...

When you have finished arranging your label, click Next. Then you can preview each recipient's label and make any individual changes.

Replicate labels

You can copy the layout of the first label to the other labels on the page by clicking the button below.

┌─────────────────────┐
│   Update all labels │
└─────────────────────┘

> ➢ To print the next address on each label, press the "Update all labels" button.
>
>   ✍ You can also use this button to apply formatting or field composition changes to all other labels.
>
> ➢ Use the preview (Next: Preview...) to check and then print it out in a new document.

Step 4 of 6

→ Next: Preview your labels

← Previous: Select recipients

That's the way it has to be. Insert «Address block» in the first field, «Next Record» and «Address block» in the next field so that the next address will be printed:

««Address»»	«Next Record» «AddressBlock»	«Next Record» «AddressBlock»
«Next Record» «AddressBlock»	«Next Record» «AddressBlock»	«Next Record» «AddressBlock»
«Next Record» «AddressBlock»	«Next Record» «AddressBlock»	«Next Record» «AddressBlock»

> ➢ Now the label is set up and you can print or save the label sheet.

18.4 Save Labels

> With "Previous..." you can go back and make changes at any time or format the address block differently, e.g. centered or insert an upper paragraph spacing.

The work should be saved when everything is perfectly set up:

> Select Save as normal for this function.

> ↳ Do not save a printout to a file because you can re-create it at any time, but save the label sheet!

> ↳ It is advisable to assign the label number as the file name.

> ↳ If you save all labels together in one folder, you will find them again without any problems.

There is no need to re-set the labels each time, you only need to open the saved file.

18.5 Envelopes and individual Labels

So far, we've handled the mail merge. Serial printing saves a lot of work e.g. with circulars to all club members or to create advertising mailings.

18.5.1 Envelope or Label

Sometimes only a single letter should be printed, for example to a new member of the association.

- either you use an envelope with a viewing window and put your return address very small over the address, as we did with our exercise letter, or

- you can print individual labels or a single envelope without having to write the address twice. Good for envelopes without viewing window.

18.5.2 Select an Address

- You can return to the serial print commands at any time on the Mailings tab.

- In "Edit recipient list" you can only tick the desired data set:

Edit
Recipient List

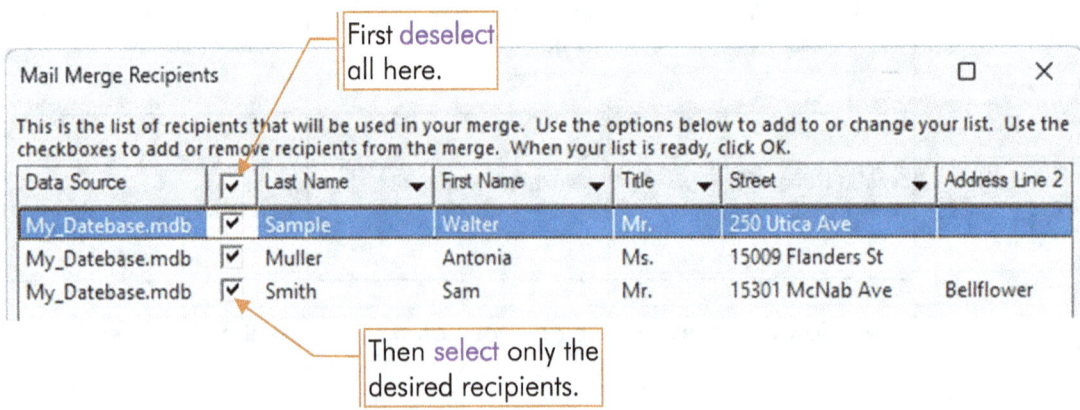

♦ With "Finish & Merge" you can also select which data set is to be printed.

Finish & Merge ⌄

Finish

 If you do not want to print a label in the upper left corner, e.g., in order to consume a label sheet bit by bit, simply crop the address in the preview (select it and [Ctrl]-x) and insert it at the desired label position.

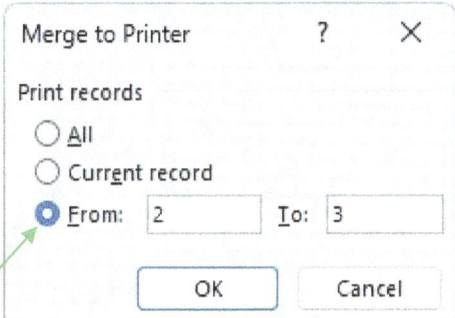

| Merge to Printer | ? | ✕ |

Print records

○ All
○ Current record
◉ From: [2] To: [3]

[OK] [Cancel]

Specify the Current record or a range.

18.6 Envelopes

18.6.1 Envelope Handmade

The simple practical solution for printed envelopes is to set up the envelope as a normal file:

♦ for example, use your envelopes paper format without a window and place the address in a document with same size as envelope in a text box (Insert/Text Box) so that it can be moved easily or the address paragraph can be moved to the desired position.

♦ For preset letters File/New and then search for "Envelopes".

♦ The address will be copied from the letter and inserted into the envelope, then if necessary save the envelope for later use with "Save as" in a separate "Envelopes" folder.

    ✍ In the same way, you can equip an envelope document set up in this way with mail merge fields instead of a specific address in order to print envelopes directly from the database.

18.6.2 The Envelope Print-function

This Word function is available instead of the manual work described above:

➢ You could first open a finished letter, select the address and copy it,

➢ then select Envelopes on the Mailings tab and paste the previously copied address using the following menu.

Envelopes   Labels   Start Mail Merge ⌄

Create

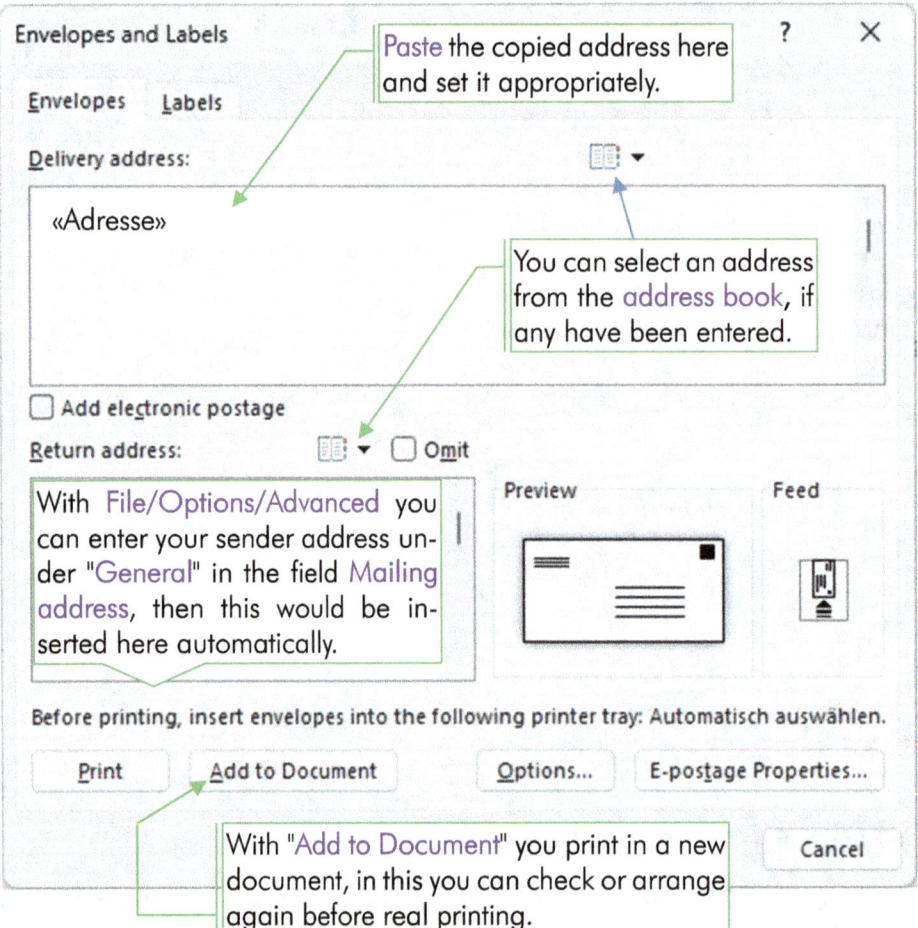

Paste the copied address here and set it appropriately.

You can select an address from the address book, if any have been entered.

With File/Options/Advanced you can enter your sender address under "General" in the field Mailing address, then this would be inserted here automatically.

With "Add to Document" you print in a new document, in this you can check or arrange again before real printing.

♦ Observe the preview on which you can also click, e.g. to specify the position of the address field when printing in a menu.

♦ Various envelopes and label formats can be selected for options.

♦ Use the Envelopes tab for envelopes, the Labels tab for label changes or the Labels button:

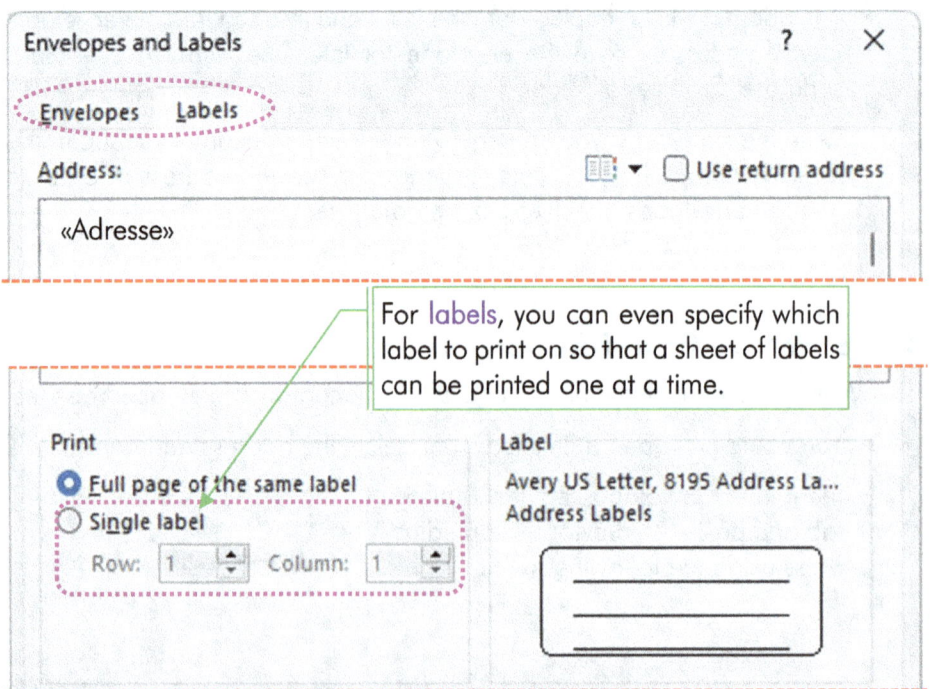

For labels, you can even specify which label to print on so that a sheet of labels can be printed one at a time.

18.7 Print Business Cards

It is also possible to create business cards if labels can already be printed. The graphic possibilities of Word are amazing.

Perfect cards can be created with colored pre-printed business cards which can be easily separated by a perforation. Measure the cards and use similar labels, especially those of the same height if there is no template.

➢ Start a new, blank document.

➢ The simplest way to print such cards is the command discussed earlier for mailing-envelopes:

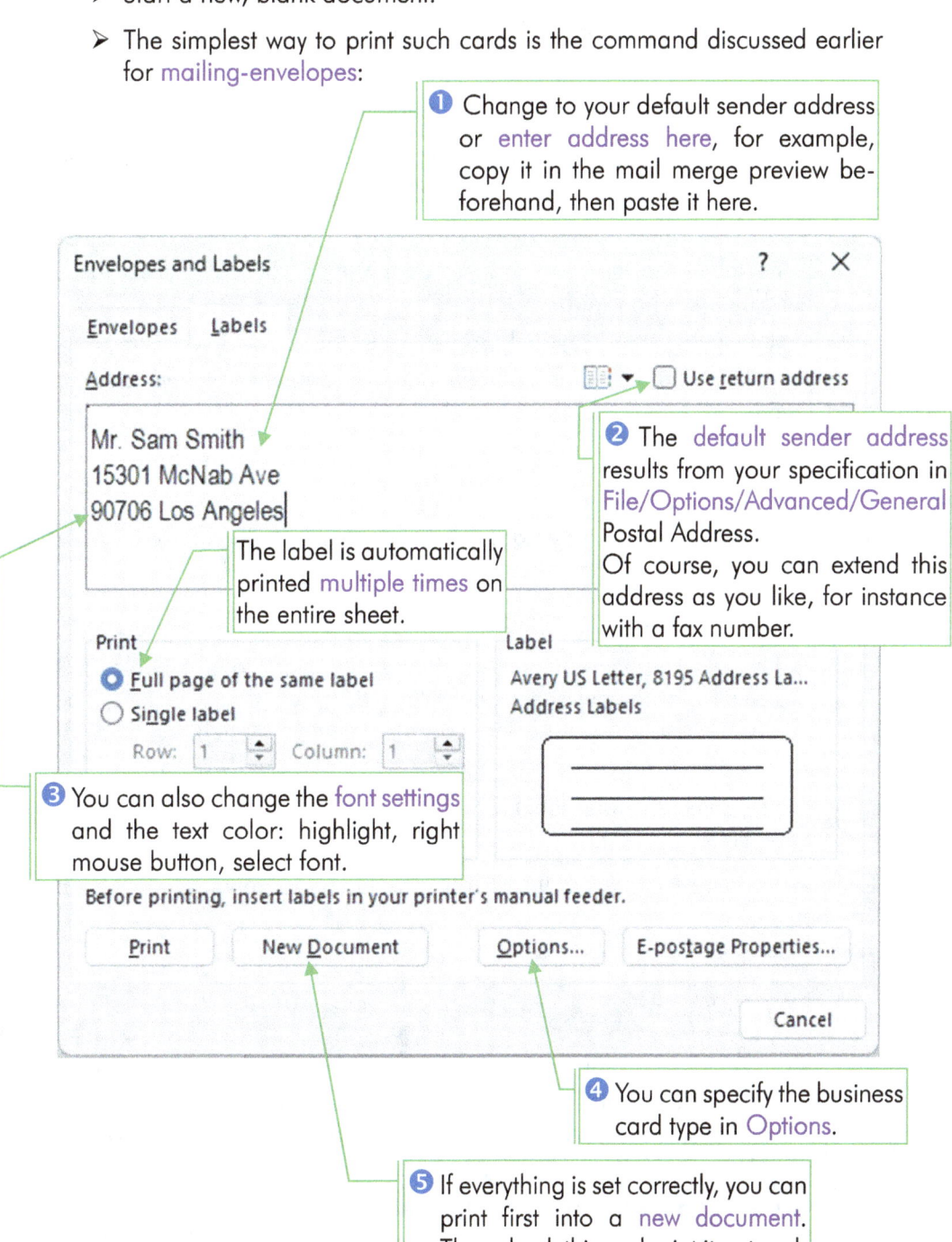

❶ Change to your default sender address or enter address here, for example, copy it in the mail merge preview beforehand, then paste it here.

Envelopes and Labels   ?   ✕

Envelopes   Labels

Address: ☐ Use return address

Mr. Sam Smith
15301 McNab Ave
90706 Los Angeles

❷ The default sender address results from your specification in File/Options/Advanced/General Postal Address.
Of course, you can extend this address as you like, for instance with a fax number.

The label is automatically printed multiple times on the entire sheet.

Print
◉ Full page of the same label
◯ Single label
   Row: 1   Column: 1

Label
Avery US Letter, 8195 Address La...
Address Labels

❸ You can also change the font settings and the text color: highlight, right mouse button, select font.

Before printing, insert labels in your printer's manual feeder.

Print   New Document   Options...   E-postage Properties...

Cancel

❹ You can specify the business card type in Options.

❺ If everything is set correctly, you can print first into a new document. Then check this and print it out real.

You will receive a text that you can finally save and format as described in the next section.

18.7.1 Design Business Cards

Resize:

With the prefabricated cards, you only need to specify the type again. If you cut your own cards or if the type is not available, either select a suitable standard type or set the label manually.

You receive a table filled with your data. The table commands allow you to adjust the format very easily afterward.

➢ Make a test printout on smear paper and place over the business card paper.

Adjust the columns and rows of the table manually until everything fits:

➢ Select row or column, right mouse button and enter an exact value for table properties. Systematically compare test printouts to get closer to the original.

➢ If the table size fits your business card paper, you can save it as a template for further work.

➢ If you want to create a new business card, access it and only exchange the entry, such as a new phone number, with the Replace at start command.

Change Design:

Secondly, the text of the business card should be optimized. The way to recreate the label template is much more cumbersome than the following:

➢ Make the first label appealing:

✎ Use all your knowledge, e.g. font size, color, italic or bold, text inverted or embellished with WordArt, small caps, locked, line spacing, special characters, graphic elements such as lines or triangles, etc.

➢ Finally, select this one label, copy it with [Ctrl]-c and paste it into the other fields with [Ctrl]-v.

Only copy when everything really fits! This only becomes apparent after a test printout.

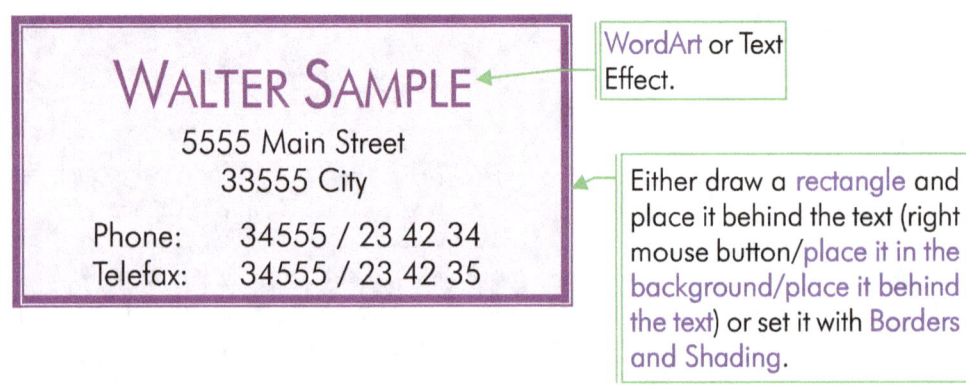

WordArt or Text Effect.

Either draw a rectangle and place it behind the text (right mouse button/place it in the background/place it behind the text) or set it with Borders and Shading.

Part Six

Other

Using Templates, Creating Forms, Calculations in Tables and a Macro

19. The Templates of Word

Are finished layout templates only at the final stage? Sure, because it's too easy to use these templates. In addition, basic knowledge of the style sheets is essential, because the templates are also built on the style sheets.

♦ Document templates are preformatted texts that save you the hassle of setting up and help you create professionally designed documents.

19.1 For a new Text

When you start a new text, you can select a template by File/New:

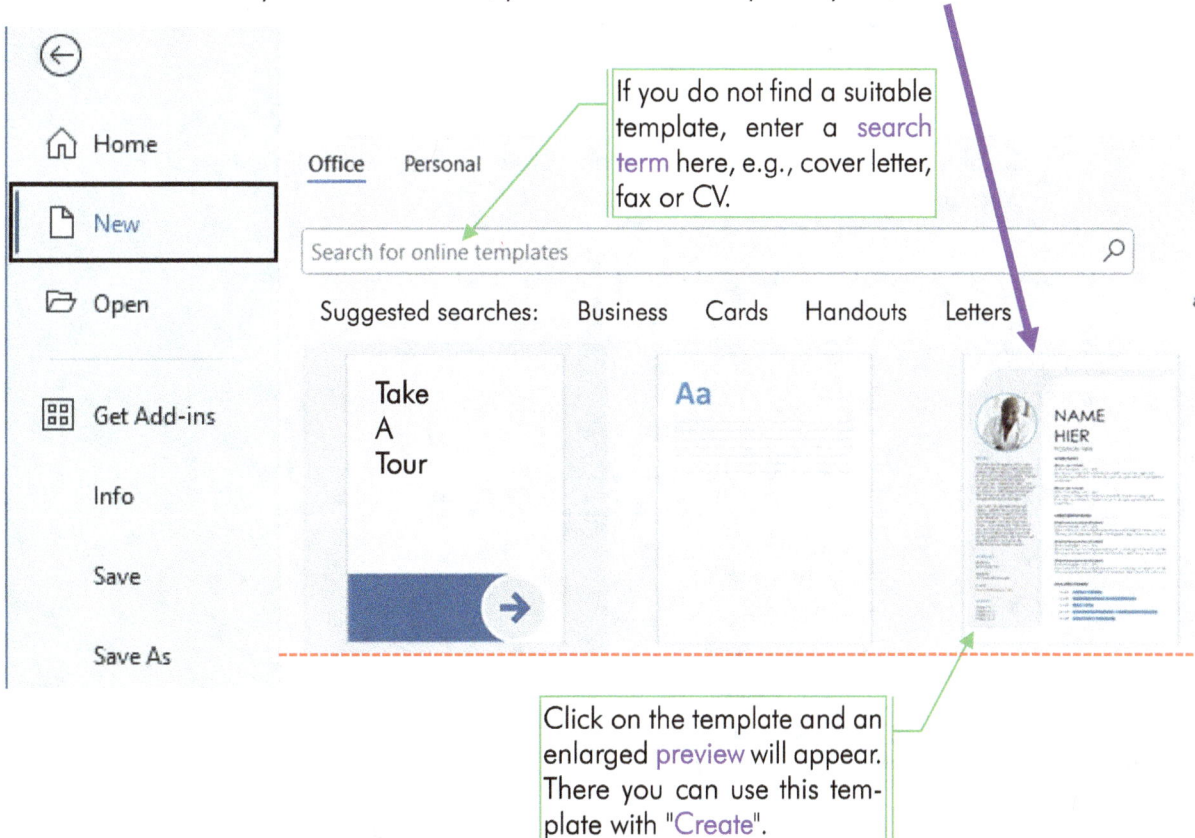

If you do not find a suitable template, enter a search term here, e.g., cover letter, fax or CV.

Click on the template and an enlarged preview will appear. There you can use this template with "Create".

➢ Start some new documents using a template to view them, then close them without saving.

19.1.1 The File Extension

Templates must be different from normal documents: Documents have the file extension docx for the document while templates can be recognized by the file extension dotx of the document layout.

19.2 The Effect of a Document Template

♦ The page format has already been set, e.g. for the multi-column leaflets brochure.

♦ The sample text in the document is formatted correctly so that you only have to overwrite it with your text and at the same time the instructions on how to use the template.

Document templates help you to create documents with a professional design.

Formatting using Style sheets:

♦ Overwriting the instructions will completely remove them. Take a good look beforehand, as you will have to format your own texts in the same way by selecting the correct style sheets.

  ✎ If necessary, open one template twice, one original for viewing and another template for customizing with your own texts.

  ✎ It is necessary to familiarize yourself with the pre-programmed style sheets in order to be able to set your own texts.

Tips for the Style sheets:

♦ Display Style menu, click on text paragraphs and study, which style sheets were used for which texts.

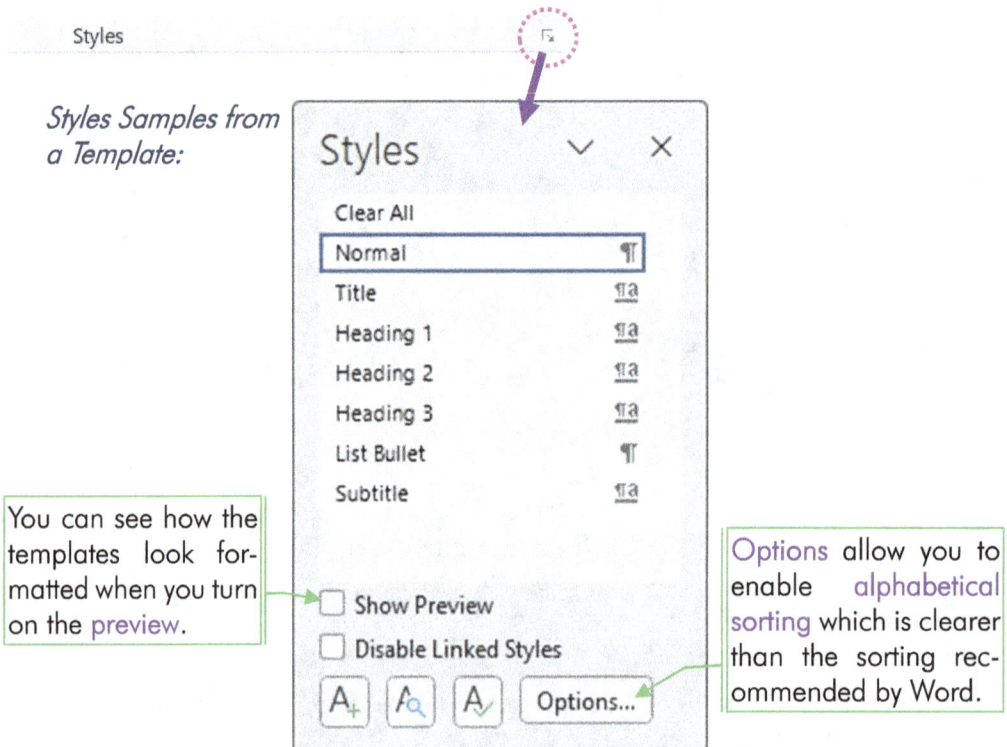

Styles Samples from a Template:

You can see how the templates look formatted when you turn on the preview.

Options allow you to enable alphabetical sorting which is clearer than the sorting recommended by Word.

19.3 For an existing Text

♦ You can only select a document template if you start a new Text.

🖋 If text already exists, copy it from the old text into the newly started text with a template.

> Already existing texts can be assigned Themes in which the style sheets have been preset.

➢ Select Design/Themes for the Text:

A theme does not change the background color, unless a background color is uniquely selected for Page Color, that background color will be updated to match the themes.

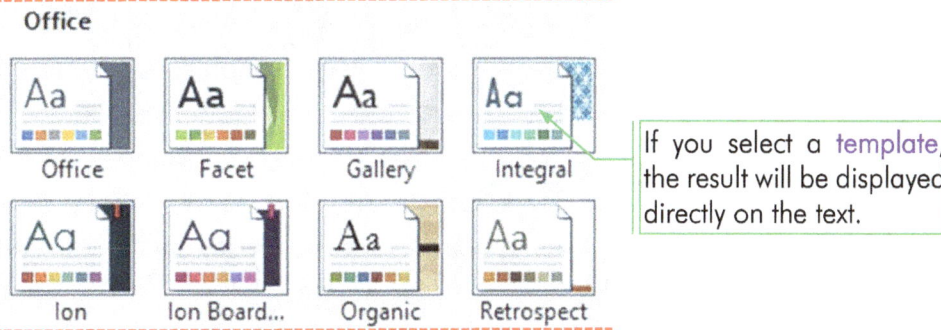

If you select a template, the result will be displayed directly on the text.

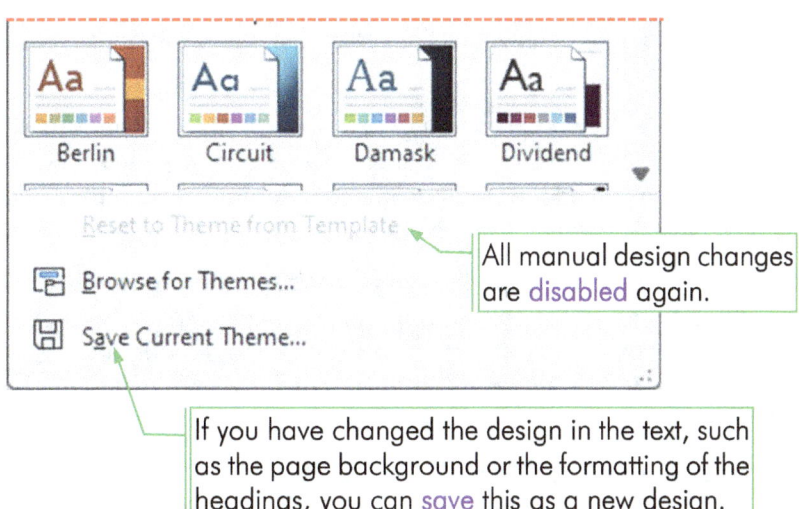

All manual design changes are disabled again.

If you have changed the design in the text, such as the page background or the formatting of the headings, you can save this as a new design.

♦ In the middle, different color and font combinations can be selected for "document formatting"; for colors, other color combinations, the effects, such as a shadow or lowered do only apply to drawn objects.

19.4 Summary

The following interesting options are available:

♦ the practical way to start a new text with a template in the case of File/New,

♦ Assign a new design (new color and font combinations) to a text with draft/design, and

♦ Select a colored page background or gradient, a pattern, or a photo as the page background for Page Color.

19.5 Create Fax Template Exercise

➢ Select a new document and a fax template, enter "fax" for this under File/New at the top search field for templates.

➢ Set up the document with your data ready for use.

➢ If you want to save the created faxes after sending them, you can copy it later with "Save as".

Because you need to set up your documents only once and can reproduce them as often as you like with save as files, it is usually better to preset your own files without templates. Of course, you can start new documents, for example, with the templates to get some ideas for the design of a letter.

19.6 Business Card Exercise

➢ File/New and search for "business cards" under "Search for online templates", numerous diverse business cards are found.

↳ As soon as you click on a card, note the display showing which label formats the respective business cards are suitable for.

➢ Select a template and the new business card document will open. Many designs have preset fields.

↳ If you overwrite these fields one by one in the upper left business card with your data, whereby one field must always be marked exactly, so simply click on it, then the changes will be automatically adopted into the following ones if you use the [Tab] button.

↳ However, formatting, e.g., the font or size, is not automatically applied, but you do not have to apply the changes to all other entries manually, because there are styles set up for the various areas that you can use to create each business card automatically can be adjusted.

Alternatives have been described on p. 30 and p. 109.

20. Create a Form

The Mask (e.g. Name, Street, etc.) of a Form should always be the same. The data can only be entered in prepared fields.

This is achieved by the following steps:

♦ The mask is saved and protected as a new document template.

✎ Open a new text based on this template if you want to fill out the form.

✎ The protection means that only the fields can be filled in, while the mask itself cannot be changed.

Fields are inserted as placeholders so that data can be entered into the mask.

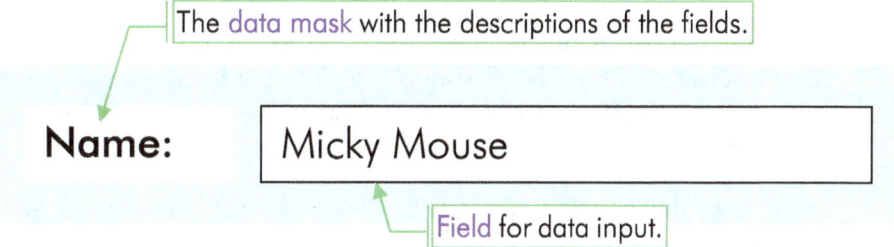

The data mask with the descriptions of the fields.

Name: Micky Mouse

Field for data input.

You can use forms in these two ways:

♦ You print out the form to send it. You enter the returned data into the computer, usually not into the form, but into a database for evaluation.

♦ The forms are filled out directly on the computer, e.g. for test persons of a market research institute invited by the street or you send the forms electronically as a file which is attached to an email and receive the answers in the same way.

20.1 Create the Mask

We will prepare a membership application for the exercise. We need a new document template and the Form creation commands.

➢ Start a new empty document. Either under File/Options or right mouse button on the ribbon bar at top, there you can by "Customize the Ribbon" activate on right side the developer tools.

> ☑ Review
> ☑ View
> ☑ Developer
> ☑ Add-ins

✎ If necessary, switch to "All commands" under "Select commands" if the developer tools are not displayed on the left.

➢ Enter "German Association Club" as the heading, then save straight away, but select our exercise folder under "More Options" and "Browse", then "Word Template" as the file type below:

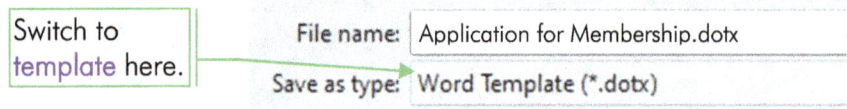

Word automatically switches to the templates folder:

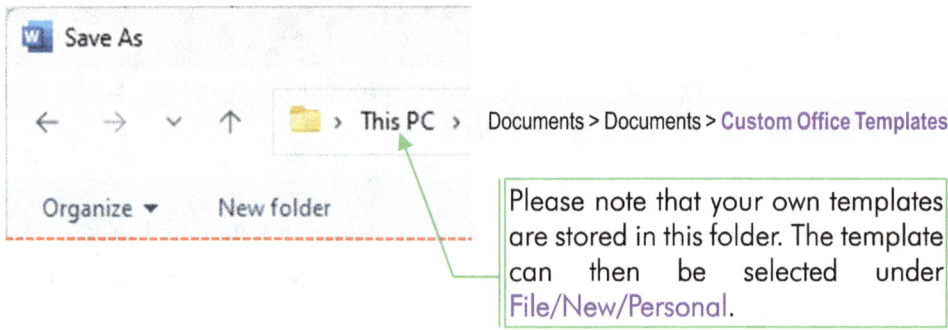

Please note that your own templates are stored in this folder. The template can then be selected under File/New/Personal.

➢ The Microsoft templates were saved actually in this folder:

C:\user\user name\documents\custom office templates

> Note that your own templates are saved in this folder. Then the template can be selected at File/New/Personal. Don't forget to create your own or modified templates when backing up your data! If you don't find the folder, search in the windows explorer the file name.
>
> Because of the ongoing chaos with Microsoft's suggestions, we still recommend saving in a self-created folder on your own hard drive. Then you know exactly where your data is stored and can't forget it when backing up your data.

◆ Now you can edit a document template that has the extension dotx when it was saved. This document template can be edited like a normal text.

For Practice:

➢ Set the paper size to letter 8 ½ x 11 inch, landscape, margins normal.

➢ Write and format the header of the form similarly:

German Association Club
for the promotion of the Associations

Chairman: Prof. Dr. J.J. James, Prof. Dr. Ben Bigman
Administrative office: Markstreet 57 - 99999 Thousandcity
Phone: 012345/345345 - Fax: 012345/345346
Application for Membership

20.2 Checkboxes as first Icons

To insert fields, you need the Form toolbar.

➢ Complete and adjust the position with tabs using the ruler:

as a full member   as an irregular member

Two boxes should be ticked in front of the two-member alternatives.

➢ On the previously activated Developer Tools tab you will find the form icons: Place the cursor in front of "as a regular member", then insert a checkbox, and also in front of "as an irregular member".

The Result: ☐·as·a·full·member   →   ☐·as·an·irregular·member¶

➢ Note the Design Mode button, which allows you to switch to the normal view or to the draft mode for editing the buttons.

The form mask must be protected at the latest during the last saving, but only when the form is really ready to be filled in to make sure that only the fields can be filled in from now on and not the form itself can be changed because this is the whole purpose of a form.

20.3 Protect Form

➢ Press the "Restrict Editing" Icon:

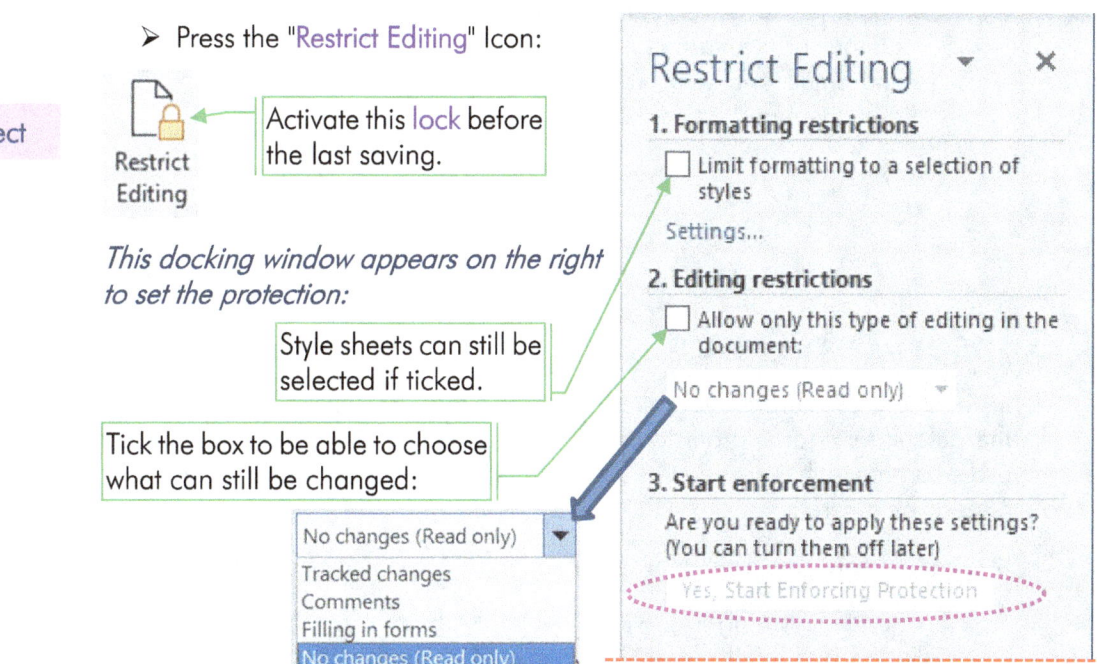

Select "Fill in Forms".

↳ This means that the form can only be changed if the document template is opened again as a template. However, only the form fields may be filled in for texts based on the template.

> Do not forget to apply Protection with "Yes, Start Enforcing Protection", if you then confirm the password question empty, then no password is required to remove the protection again! So always with a password.

➢ Try out whether you can still change something, such as delete text, add or fill in fields.

20.4 Re-Edit Form

➢ Save and Close the Text.

➢ File/New, then switch to Personal and select the template you just created: "*Application for Membership*".

➢ Try changing the text and filling in the boxes.

  ✎ Please note that due to the protection of the template, the template "*Application for Membership*" was not opened either, but a new, not yet saved text with the content of the template.

➢ Close this sample text without saving it, then open the document again as a template: File/Open/Application for Membership.dotx and lift the protection so we can complete the template:

  ✎ To do this, click on the "Stop Protection" icon again at the Developer Tools tab, at the very bottom of the Restrict editing section you will find small and well hidden "Stop Protection", click there and unlock with the password.

20.5 Insert Text Fields

In the previous exercise, you already learned that we can no longer change the default texts for a protected form. Special text fields are inserted so that users can make their text entries, in which a frequently used template text can already be entered.

Let's continue with the form. Now you need a text form field after each question.

➢ Write the following text, with a decimal tabulator for the input, a right-aligned one for the specifications, and a left-aligned one for the text form fields to align the columns appropriately.

➢ Then move the cursor to the position and insert the text form fields:

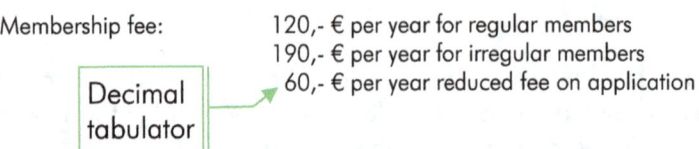

Membership fee: 120,- € per year for regular members
                    190,- € per year for irregular members
                    60,- € per year reduced fee on application

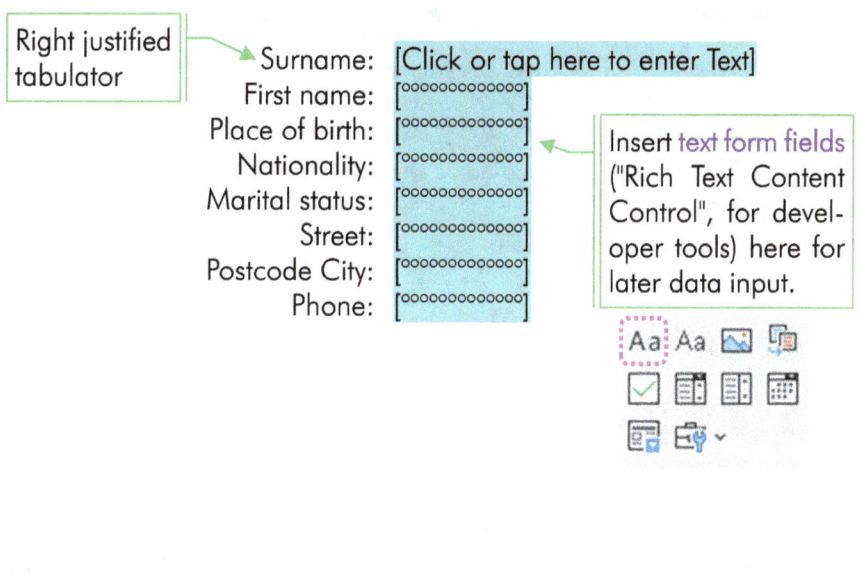

Place, Date: Signature

20.6 The Options

Aa Aa

Generally, there are two different text fields, therefore, a line break can be blocked at the right "only text", i.e. only single line entries are possible.

♦ Any text form field can be set: click, then select Properties at the top of the toolbar.

⬦ Different settings are available depending on whether you have selected a text form field or a box.

📝 Design Mode

⬚ Properties

📋 Group ⌄

Setting options for checkboxes:

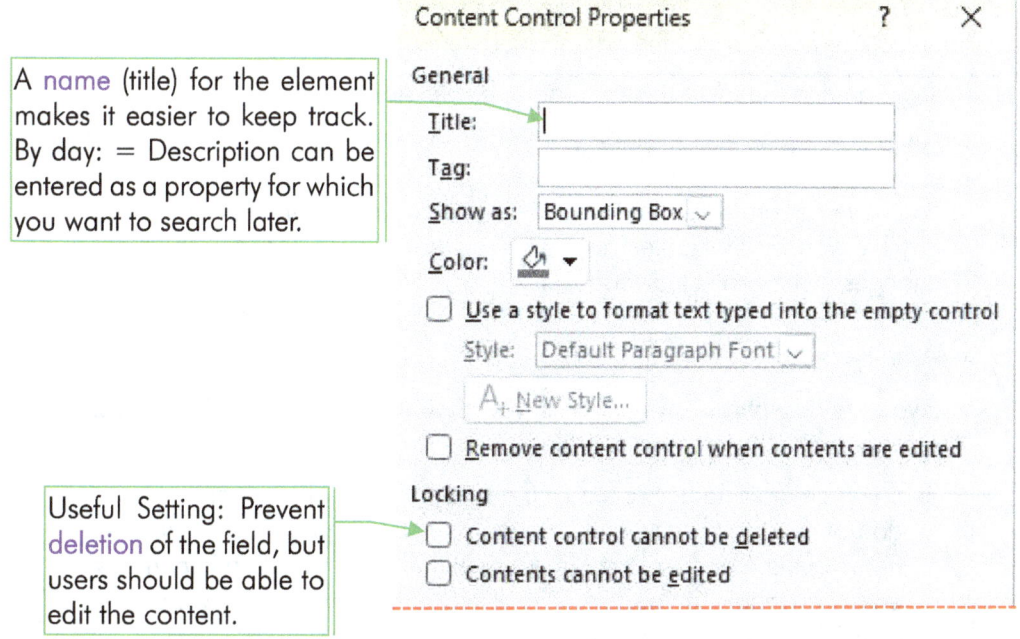

You can set the default settings at the bottom of the menu:

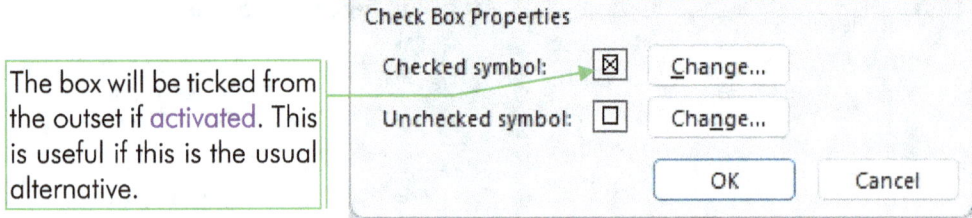

The box will be ticked from the outset if activated. This is useful if this is the usual alternative.

To the Style Sheets:

You can assign a Style sheet to save formatting work, for example, a new style sheet for the text fields.

♦ If you use two different styles for checkboxes and text form fields, the formatting for them could be changed at any time, no matter how many such elements were used, for example, text form fields in this style could be capitalized.

     ✎ So that this style does not apply to the entire paragraph, but only to the box or form field, use Character as the style type instead of paragraph.

♦ However, if you use the same style as the text, the boxes will always have the same formatting as the surrounding text.

20.7 Enter Data

If the form is saved as a document template and was previously protected.

➢ Protect the template, save and close it.

You can work now with it as follows:

➢ Press File, then New, then Up to "Personal".

➢ Select the new form as the document template.

➢ Try changing the text - this should not be possible.

➢ Fill in the form with your data.

> You have not protected the template if you can still change the default texts! If you cannot enter any text, you had ticked the option "No changes (write-protected/read-only)".

New Members:

♦ If you are accepting new members, you should save each application as a separate file, print it out and file it.

     ✎ If you create a folder called e.g. membership applications, then you do not need to specify membership in each file name, but rather the name of the new member, then you will find an application later more easily, especially if you use precise file names, e.g. *"Muller, Martin, Munich"* or *"Muller, Eva, Berlin".*

20.8 Drop-down Form Field

♦ A drop-down form field is used when you select a font in Word: a list of presets will fold down as soon as you press the arrow.

    ↳ Dropdown form fields are similar and possible input texts can be selected from a list.

To the next Exercise:

➢ Open the exercise text Hfee.dot. You can use File Save As to make a copy into your exercise folder.

    ↳ Note that this should remain a dot template file, so save it as a Word template

    ↳ in the current Word format dotx in order to have all options available to confirm the message.

Add a combination field with this icon after "The reason is:".

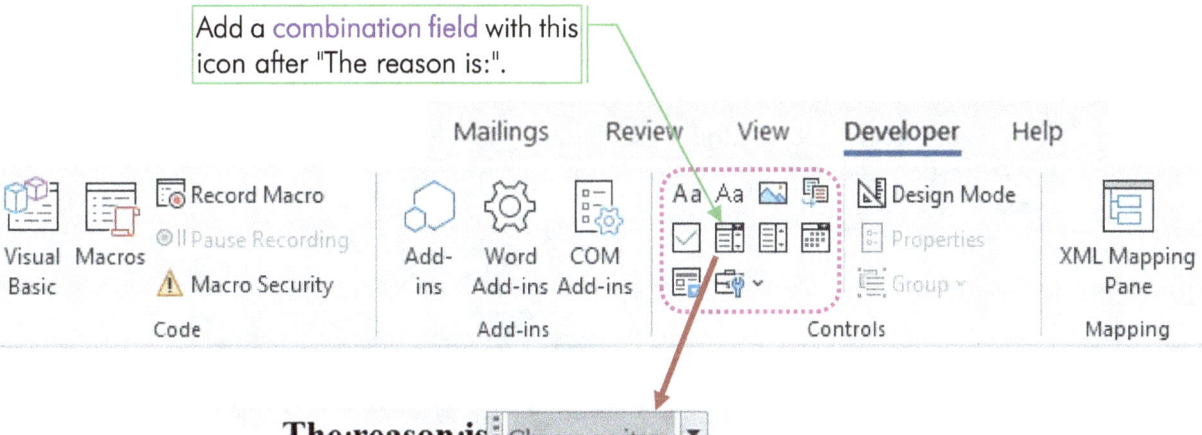

Now the default texts must be created:

➢ Click on the field and select Properties at the top of Developer Tools.

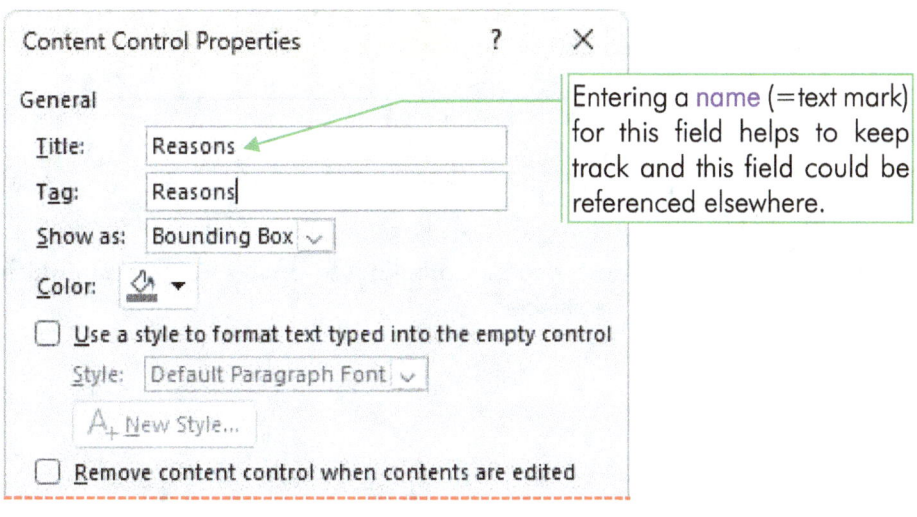

Entering a name (=text mark) for this field helps to keep track and this field could be referenced elsewhere.

Now you have to enter the texts that should be available for selection:

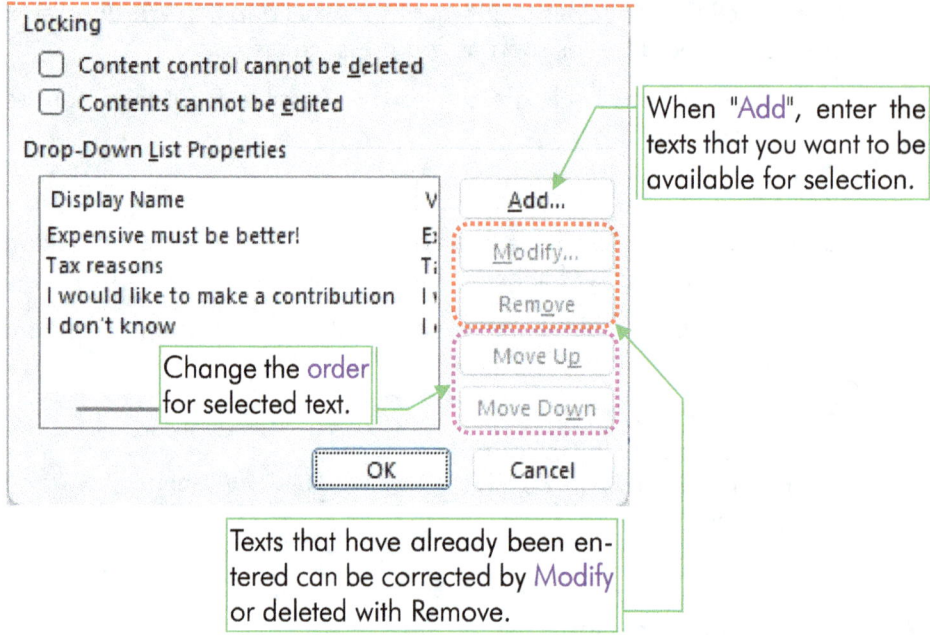

When "Add", enter the texts that you want to be available for selection.

Change the order for selected text.

Texts that have already been entered can be corrected by Modify or deleted with Remove.

Miscellaneous:

➢ If you are not in Design Mode, you can test the field by pressing the arrow and selecting one of the prefabricated texts.

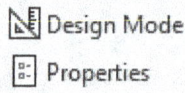

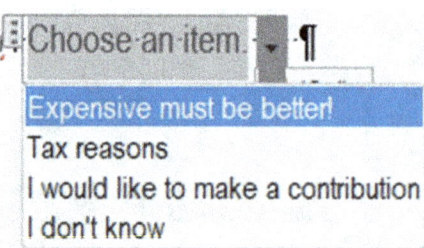

➢ Format the legal basis paragraph at the end with smaller font so that there is space to add fields for name and address (street, zip code, city) after "The reason is",

➢ then another date selection button and signature,

➢ finally, save as a Template.

To complete the form:

➢ The Form is ready to use by protecting and saving the document template again.

➢ Subsequently, new texts can be started based on this template, in which only the fields can be selected.

21. Calculations

In Word, Calculations can only be performed in a single Table.

- ♦ In a Table, you can, for instance, calculate the total, the value-added tax or a discount amount.

- ♦ Miscalculations are now a thing of the past, because Word doesn't miscalculate any more than a calculator does,

- ♦ annoying recalculation and re-calculation after additions also: right mouse button and "Update Field" is sufficient.

21.1 First Example

The final prices are to be determined in a dealer price list:

Price Example for 4-Wheeled Car, Model XK Turbo	
Base price:	19,877.56 €
Special equipment for Steering wheel:	666.89 €
Lockable entrance doors:	2,222.99 €
Milled out trunk opening:	3,444.78 €
Safety package: ABS, Airbag:	4,555.99 €
Clean package: Shower curtain, Mudguards, Windshield cleaners:	1,987.65 €
Metallic paint:	1,898.89 €
F i n a l p r i c e :	

The sum is eventually missing:

➢ Open the "Car Center Nirvana" exercise, save in your exercise folder, and set the cursor to the final price, then switch to the Layout tab:

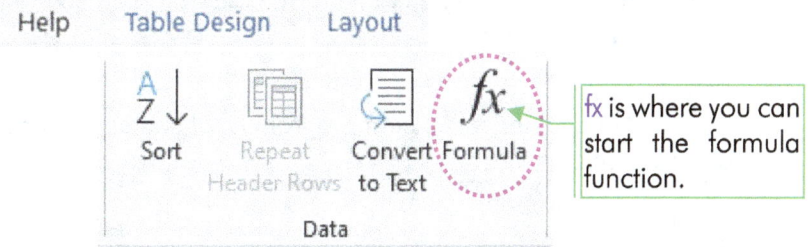

fx is where you can start the formula function.

Select the formula and the number format in the formula menu:

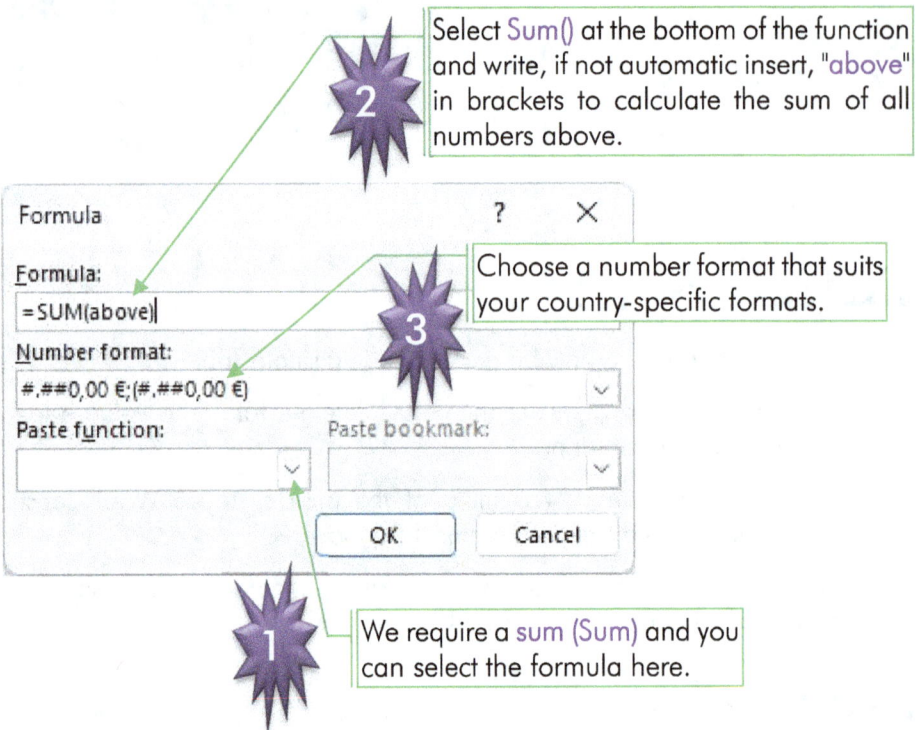

2 Select Sum() at the bottom of the function and write, if not automatic insert, "above" in brackets to calculate the sum of all numbers above.

3 Choose a number format that suits your country-specific formats.

1 We require a sum (Sum) and you can select the formula here.

That was it. Your computer is ticking correctly if you also see € 34,654.75. If not, check the following rules for calculations.

21.2 Update and Causes of errors

The value can be updated very easily when changes are made:

> ➢ press the right mouse button over the number, select Update Fields.

> ➢ The formula can be displayed instead of the result using the right mouse button and field functions on/off. The system will display Sum (above) with the selected number format.

Update

Some of the most common causes of errors in Word calculations:

♦ Important: The last row of calculations must not contain connected cells!

♦ Blank cells must be filled with "0" for addition and with "1" for multiplication.

♦ Additional calculations in a table lead to incorrect results.

    ✎ Therefore, in separate tables or with the "pocket calculator" (start/calculator) will manually create or immediately use a calculation program.

Error sources

    MS Excel or another calculation program is, of course, better suited for extensive calculations.

21.3 Kindergarten

A somewhat larger example: For spatial planning, the usable square meters are to be determined from the room dimensions. The areas occupied by the heaters and cubicles must be subtracted, which should be done automatically.

New construction of a day nursery and crèche:

Pre-calculations: Square footage - unusable space			
Kiga-Gr. 1	**Length**	**Width**	**Surface area**
Room	305	276	
Cabinet 1	-57	48	
Cabinet 2	-36	9	
Heater 1	-60	2	
Heater 2	-12	89	
		Result:	

All information in inches

➢ Open the "Kindergarten" exercise.

➢ Enter the following formula for the first Area: = Product(left).

fx
Formel

    ↳ you can copy the "left", insert a formula Product, and delete the rest of Sum(left) suggested by Word, or simply overwrite Sum manually with Product(left).

    ↳ If you select 0 as the numerical format, the number will be displayed without decimal places.

➢ Copy this formula and paste it into the following rows, then click right mouse button and Update field in the copied formulas.

➢ Add to Result = Sum(above).

> The product is automatically negative because the minus was entered in the Length column and the same formula =Sum(above) can be used.

Conversion to feet:

With such large numbers, it is common to specify them in feet; we can also convert inches to feet in Word with a little trick: using text marks and cross-references to these text marks.

➢ Add another column on the right.

➢ Mark the Surface area at Room, then Insert/Bookmark and define this value as Bookmark Room.

➢ Now click in the new empty cell to the right and insert a formula in Layout.

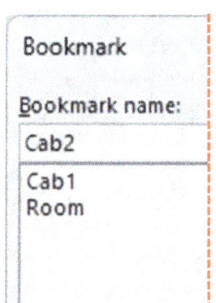
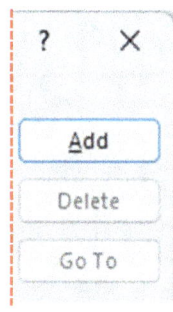

> In the formula menu, write "=", then insert the Bookmark under "Paste Bookmark" and write /12 after it, select 0 as the number format, done.

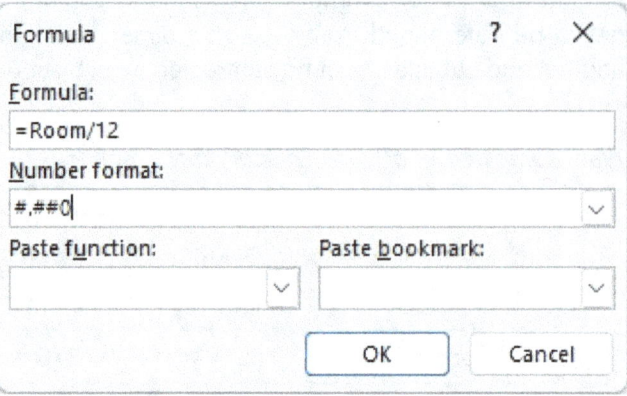

> In the next lines, first set the result as a bookmark, then insert a formula with this bookmark and /12 to the right of it.

> In the Sum line insert a Sum(above), ready is the column with feets instead inchs.

The conversion with decimal places from inch to foot would really be too complicated for Word. Here a detour via MS Excel would be necessary, but not difficult, copying the results, pasting them into a new Excel table, inserting the formula "convert" in the cell to the right and specifying it when converting from in to ft. Then copy this formula into the following lines and finally copy the results and transfer them back to Word.

A short summary:

As you can see, a lot of other calculations are possible! Even references to calculated values are possible to insert a result elsewhere.

♦ To do this, mark the value with a bookmark: Insert/Bookmark,

♦ then it can be cross-referenced elsewhere: Insert/Cross Reference or References/Cross Reference,

   ✍ wherein with "References to: Bookmark content" the formula result is inserted.

Notes: ....

....

....

....

....

....

....

....

....

....

....

....

....

....

22. A Macro

Normally, you execute a single command. These commands are often repeated, so you must repeatedly enter identical command sequences.

Word can do this for you by saving these commands as Macros. When this Macro is executed, Word repeats the entire process exactly as you entered the commands.

For what Macros? Some application examples:

- ◆ Often used to reformat databases or to adapt texts created in other programs to Word:
  - ↳ to replace control characters that Word does not recognize with the appropriate formatting.
- ◆ This can also be done with the very powerful Search and Replace command,
  - ↳ but a macro is worthwhile if reformatting is necessary regularly, e.g. because you repeatedly receive such texts from another company.
- ◆ You have purchased a color printer and would now like to convert all texts that were previously only set up in black and white to color.
  - ↳ These can be quite a few actions such as header, page numbers and headings colored, style sheet quotation with colored background and frame, bullets in a different color, etc.
  - ↳ Of course, the changes are entered in the style sheets, but instead of performing these steps manually for each text, a macro can be created to make the changes in the style sheets.
  - ↳ You execute this macro as soon as you retrieve a text, and the style sheets will be customized in color.
- ◆ If the mail merge function cannot be used because the data is to be compiled from multiple data sources.
  - ↳ Special construction with a macro can help in this case, which is illustrated by the second example.

22.1 Create Macro

Let's assume that you bought a color printer and now you want to change the color of the over scripts to color and the previously gray frames and shades to color.

A macro is created in order to avoid having to repeat these operations for each text.

> ➢ Open the "Sample Text Macro".

We want to set the following as a Macro:

- ♦ The Headings are to be set to dark blue.

- ♦ The paragraphs with the style sheet quotation should have a dark red font and a yellow frame line.

Procedure:

> ➢ Macros can be found in the View menu and in the Developer tab:

Chapter 20.1 on page 117 describes how to activate the Developer Tools tab.

> ➢ Select Record Macro.

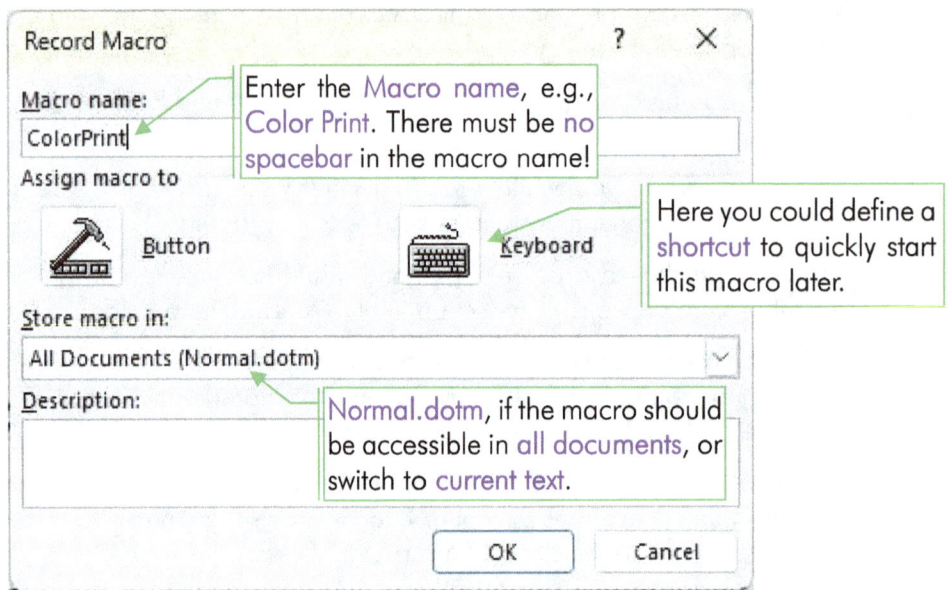

> ➢ A cassette-symbol on the mouse indicates that the macro is now being recorded, although not everyone knows music cassettes anymore.

Now do the formatting as usual, except that each step is now recorded in the Macro:

> ➢ Open the style menü, right mouse button over heading 1 in the style menu, then select blue as the font color for headings 1 and 2.

> ➢ For the style sheet Quote, select the text color red and frame color orange, then "Stop recording".

22.2 Try out Macro

The text was already formatted when the macro was created.

Macros

➢ In order to be able to try out the macro, we have to undo the text twice to return it to its original state.

➢ Open the Macro menu, then select the Color Print macro and press Execute.

You will find your new macro in the menu and can apply one of the commands listed on the right, e.g. execute the macro again or delete it.

Now the text is automatically formatted as specified in the Macro. You can now execute this Macro in any other text.

♦ You can access the Visual Basic Editor by choosing Single Step or Edit (= Debug an error message) and change the macro from there (Visual Basic knowledge required).

22.3 Organize and Rationalize Macros

♦ The previous macro menu allows you to copy a macro to other document templates when organizing. Macros are usually saved in the document template normal.dotm.

> It is recommended that you include these templates in your backup after you have created Macros so that the Macros are not lost after a re-installation: search for normal.dotm in Windows Explorer to find this file and create a backup.

To start a macro as often as you like, it is recommended to assign a keyboard shortcut for the macro.

♦ This can either be done before recording with the Keyboard button or unfortunately very hidden in the Word options.

Assign a keyboard shortcut afterward:

➢ Select File/Options, then Customize Ribbon on the left, by "choose commands from:" choose Macros and you can mark your macro and then Customize on the bottom right for Keyboard shortcuts.

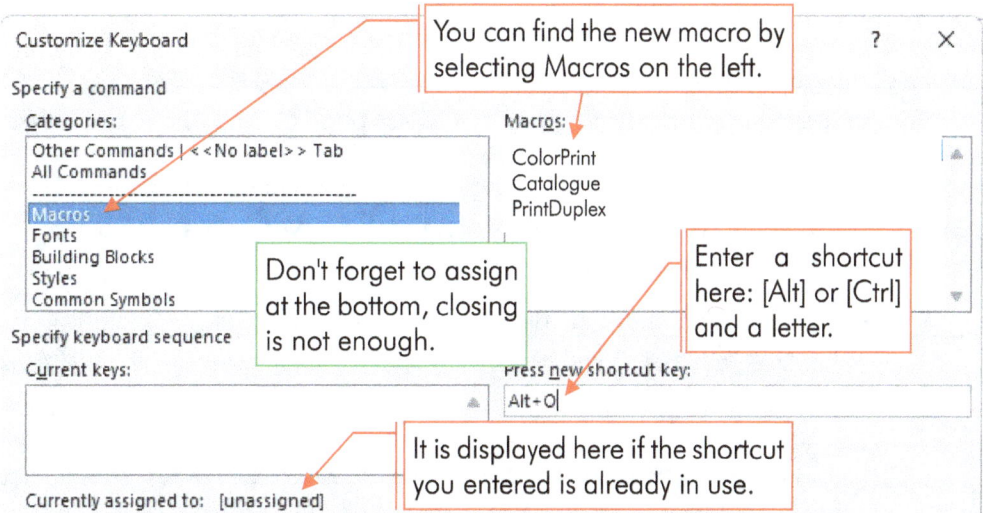

22.4 Macro for Data Synchronization

- ◆ A musician association would like to update the addresses of its members once a year, correct them if necessary and post them online. For this reason, everyone is contacted and the address entry of the last calendar is printed on the letter for control.

- ◆ Because the text printed in the catalog contains not only the address but also additional information from a second database, the data for each serial letter must be taken from two different databases and this is too much for the normal serial letter function.

Create Macro[5]:

- ➢ Copy the folder Macro to MacroCopy, since we will delete data during execution, open all three texts from the copied folder MacroCopy.

Now the first address is inserted. Proceed as follows:

- ➢ Take your starting position: Place cursor in the "Letter Catalog" at the top, then Developer/Record Macro, as a name "CatalogEntry", after Ok switch to Addresses Catalog. Important: Switch at View/Switch Windows.

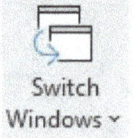

Switch Windows ⌄

- ➢ Select the first address paragraph with [Ctrl]-[Shift]-Arrow-Key, then cut this paragraph with [Ctrl]-X.

- ➢ Now switch back to the letter catalog at view/window.

- ➢ Navigate seven times down with the direction key to the address wander, highlight it down with [Ctrl]-[Shift]-Direction key and overwrite it with the current address with [Ctrl]-V.

The first address is followed by the catalog entry:

That was the first part called the address. We always choose Cut instead of Copy so that the next catalog address can be inserted using the same procedure. Now the catalog entry follows:

- ➢ Change view/window to entry catalog, again with [Ctrl]-[Shift]-direction key down, mark the first entry and cut ([Ctrl]-X) with window change back to letter catalog.

- ➢ Move 15 times down to the line "Catalogue-Entry", then press [Pos1] and mark the paragraph with [Ctrl]-[Shift]-Direction key down and insert the copied with [Ctrl]-V.

- ➢ The letter is now ready and we have entered the address and the text which we can print with the print icon.

- ➢ Finally, press [Ctrl]-[Pos1] to return to the start position, so that the next operation will run the same way, then stop recording. This also is the reason we start with the cursor at top of page and not direct at adress.

Execute Macro Multiple Times:

In this way, however, you can still execute Macro several times without Visual Basic programming knowledge:

- ➢ Just create another macro that contains the first macro, e.g. starts ten times. Assign a shortcut to this macro so that it can be started easily.

---

[5] This macro was really programmed in the 1990years by Peter Schiessl for a German music association and there over ten years helpfully used.

23. Search and Organize

We describe some ways to search for files below. This can be very useful for you because if you accidentally saved a file to the wrong folder or filename, it can be difficult to find it again.

23.1 The different search options

Open Files:

- ♦ You can search for your text in Word by File/Open, if the text you have saved last is not found here.

    ↳ Open this document amd select File/Save As and remember only the location, then cancel, close the text and serch it in the Windows Explorer in this folder and move it to the correct folder.

- ♦ In the File/Open menu, you can also select files while browsing and then rename or delete them with the right mouse button.

Search Files:

- ♦ How to search in a text is easy with Search option in MS Word and was discussed on page 72.

- ♦ This is about finding missing files,

    ↳ in Windows: right mouse button on the start icon/Search or click on the "magnifying glass" symbol at start,

    ↳ or in Word for File/Open/Browse or use the Windows Explorer.

Search in Windows Explorer:

- ♦ On the left, select the drive or folder you want to search, then enter a search term at the top, such as monthly report.

    ↳ If you select the entire drive, the file is more likely to be found, but the search takes significantly longer than if you can specify the folder approximately.

    ↳ Didn't find what you were looking for? Maybe you didn't back up locally, but rather on OneDrive, for example?

23.2 The Document Properties

♦ You can save additional information for each text in the document properties, which can be searched for later: Author, Topic, Category, etc.

♦ Select File to display or enter the properties. On the left in the command list, you will find "Info" on the current document.

   ↳ Here you can also add or change entries, simply click on an entry or go further to the advanced properties.

23.2.1 Advanced Document Properties

Well hidden, you can access the advanced document properties in the previous information menu by selecting "Show all Properties":

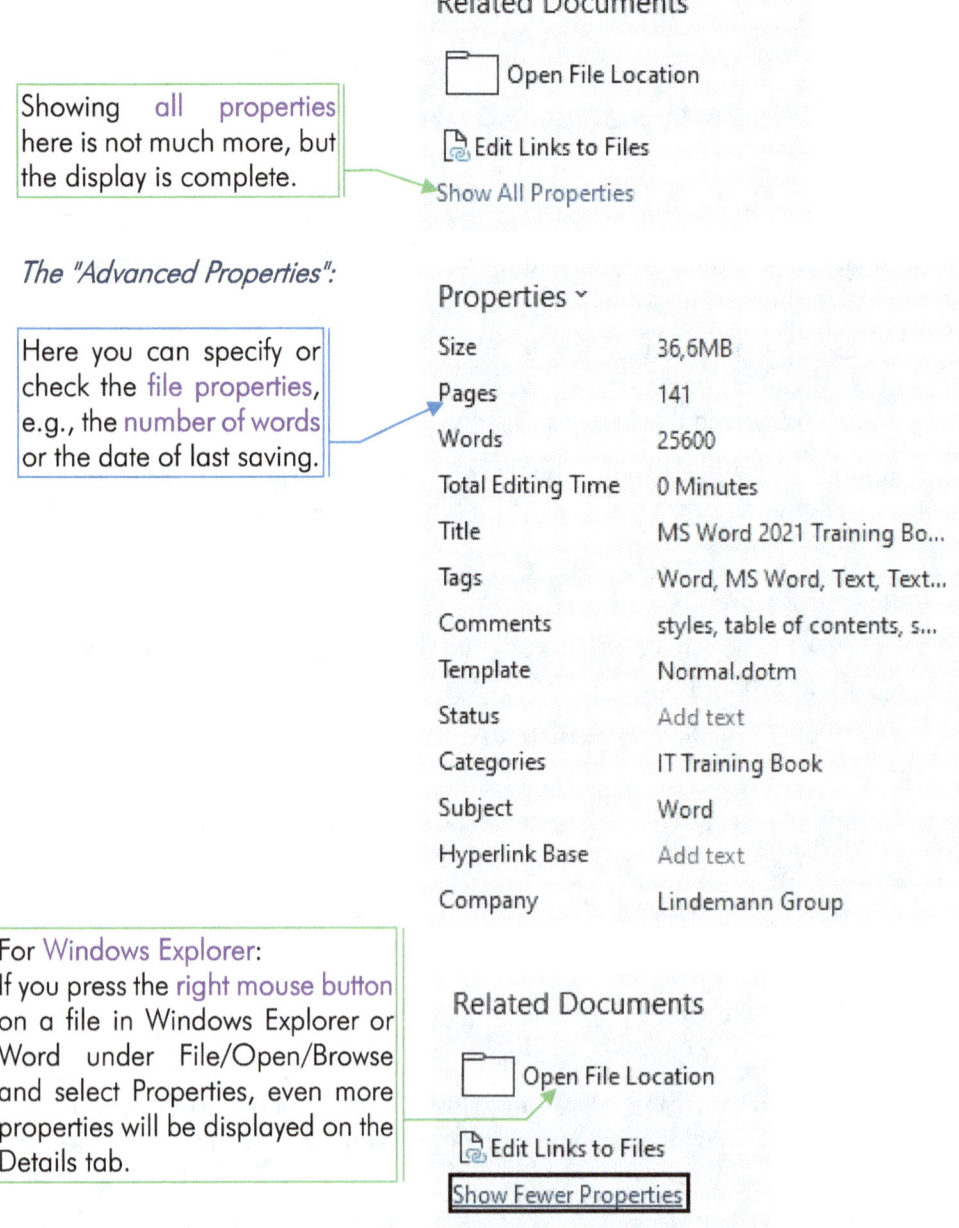

Related Documents

   📁 Open File Location

Showing all properties here is not much more, but the display is complete.

   📄 Edit Links to Files

Show All Properties

The "Advanced Properties":

Here you can specify or check the file properties, e.g., the number of words or the date of last saving.

Properties ˅

Size	36,6MB
Pages	141
Words	25600
Total Editing Time	0 Minutes
Title	MS Word 2021 Training Bo...
Tags	Word, MS Word, Text, Text...
Comments	styles, table of contents, s...
Template	Normal.dotm
Status	Add text
Categories	IT Training Book
Subject	Word
Hyperlink Base	Add text
Company	Lindemann Group

For Windows Explorer:
If you press the right mouse button on a file in Windows Explorer or Word under File/Open/Browse and select Properties, even more properties will be displayed on the Details tab.

Related Documents

   📁 Open File Location

   📄 Edit Links to Files

Show Fewer Properties

24. ShortCuts

24.1 Standard-Shortcuts

[Ctrl]-n	New Text	[Ctrl]-x	Cut out
[Ctrl]-o	Open Text	[Ctrl]-c	Copy
[Ctrl]-s	Save	[Ctrl]-v	Paste
[Ctrl]-p	Open Print menu.	F1 or Help:	Help
[Ctrl]-z	Undo		

24.2 Selected Shortcuts for longer Texts

[Ctrl]-[Pos 1]	To the beginning.
[Ctrl]-[End]	To the end of the Text.
[Ctrl]-[Return]	Insert page break.
[Ctrl]-Hyphen	Manual Hyphenation.
[Alt]	Click briefly, do not hold down: the shortcuts for menu functions are displayed at the top.
Select:	
[Shift] - Direction keys - Image buttons	Select (from the Current Cursor Position).
[Ctrl]-[Shift] -[Pos 1] / -[End]	To select from the current cursor position to the beginning or end of the text.
[Ctrl]-a	Select all.
Important Windows:	
[Ctrl]-g	Opens the Go-To window.
[Ctrl]-f	Opens the Search Window.
[Ctrl]-h	Opens the Replace Window.
Style sheets:	
[Ctrl]-[Alt]-[Shift]-s	Opens the Styles menu.

| [Alt]-1, -2, -2, -3 | Assigns the Style sheets Heading 1, 2 or 3. |

24.3 Additional Shortcuts:

Finally, we have printed a selection of Shortcuts. You can find a complete compilation in the Help of MS Word.

Select the Function keys:

F1   Help (or click on the Help tab or enter a search item by Search).
F4   Repeat the previous operation.
F5   Select the Go to command.
F7   Selecting the Spelling command (Check menu).
F8   Expand selection: you can select the word first, then the paragraph, the paragraph including Paragraph Selection and the whole document by pressing [F8] several times. Switch off again with [Esc].
F9   Update Fields Selection.
F12   Select the Save As command.

Select Combinations with the [Shift] key:

SHIFT-F3   Changing the upper/lower case character of the letters.
SHIFT-F4   Repeat Searches or Go to.

Useful combinations with the [Ctrl] and [Shift] keys:

CTRL-SHIFT-F5   Edit a Bookmark.
CTRL-SHIFT-F6   Go to the previous Window.
CTRL-SHIFT-F7   Update linked data in a Microsoft Word source document.
CTRL-SHIFT-F8   select in rectangular form (then press the arrow keys).
CTRL-SHIFT-F9   Cancel a Field Link.

Select Combinations with the [Alt] key:

ALT-F1   Go to next Field.
ALT-F3   Create an AutoText Entry (text must be selected).
ALT-F4   Exit Microsoft Word.
ALT-F7   Find the next spelling or grammar error.
ALT-F8   the Macro-Window appears from which a Macro can be started.
ALT-F9   Toggles between Field function/Result for all Fields.
ALT-F10   a window appears in which all graphic elements of the current page are displayed. By clicking on the eye, an element can be made invisible.
ALT-F11   View the Microsoft Visual Basic code. This window can easily be closed again with the X symbol.
Reference: MS Word Help, search for "key combinations" at the bottom of the list. Here you will find a list of all available shortcuts.

25. Index